"*I only play blackjack and baccarat because I believe you can win if you're patient. Casinos are vulnerable to negative swings. It's up to the player to seize the moment. In life, patience is said to be a virtue. But at the tables, it's the calm before the storm.*"

From an interview with a high roller

ATLANTIC CITY

CITY

BEHIND THE TABLES

John Alcamo

GOLLEHON
GRAND RAPIDS, MI

Copyright © 1991
by Gollehon Press, Inc.

ALL RIGHTS RESERVED under international and Pan-American copyright conventions.

No part of this book may be reproduced or copied in any form or by any means, including graphic, electronic, mechanical, or information and retrieval systems, without written permission of the publisher.

Newspaper or magazine writers may quote brief passages for inclusion in a feature article or review, provided full credit is given.

MANUFACTURED IN THE UNITED STATES OF AMERICA

Library of Congress Catalog Card Number: 90-81515

ISBN 0-914839-22-5
(International Standard Book Number)

Gollehon does not accept unsolicited manuscripts. Brief book proposals are reviewed.

Contents

I walked the beach alone early this morning
hoping to find you there
but,
there was no one.
The sea is a wonderful place to drown your sorrows.
Half my life
is somewhere in the Atlantic.

For Mary Stella Rossi.

The author wishes to express his appreciation to:

Roger P. Wagner, President and Chief Operating Officer, Claridge Hotel.

Glenn Lillie, Vice President of Public Affairs, Claridge Hotel.

Robert Renneisen, Jr., Executive Vice President of Marketing and Casino Operations, Claridge Hotel.

Tom Flynn and John M. Kovac, Casino Control Commission.

Professor Stephen J. Ceci, Cornell University.

Professor Charles Thompson, Kansas State University.

The Amazing Kreskin, Paul Winkworth, James "Bubbles" Peronti, Dan D'Angio, Robert Sonsini, Bill Scarduzzio, Linda November.

To Belle, for her encouragement, support, and most of all, her friendship.

A special thank you to Tom Pizzi, for introducing me to author and publisher, John Gollehon.

To the dealers, pit bosses, floorpersons, and casino workers in Atlantic City, my deepest gratitude for your cooperation.

And to Dan Heneghan, staff writer for The Press of Atlantic City, and to Phil Hevener, staff writer for Gaming & Wagering Business Magazine. Thank you, gentlemen, for your careful reading of my manuscript for accuracy.

*This Book is Dedicated
to my parents,
Victor and Mary.*

ATLANTIC CITY

CITY

BEHIND
THE TABLES

CHAPTER 1

The Land Of Oz

A caravan of cruise-controlled cars travel east along the yellow brick road: Buicks, Chevys, Mercedes, Fords, Hondas, strangers passing strangers, states passing states. Limousines with tinted-glass windows tease the imagination: "Look, it's Donald Trump." Or was it Old Blue Eyes? In all likelihood it's neither Frank nor Donald in that limo, but rather some high roller from the surrounding area who's coming to town for the weekend, the day, the hour... however long it takes to win — or lose — what you or I earn in a year.

Over 35 million people annually visit this resort town by the sea, once called "the lungs of Philadelphia." Today, tell anyone within a 300-mile radius (and there's 60 million of them) that you're going to "A.C." to take a "shot," and they know you're not talking "electrical."

Who are these adventure seekers and where do they come from? They're young and old, thirtysomething, the rich and famous, the couple next door, the haves and have nots. The guy with a couple of hundred dollars in his pocket looking for a night out.

1

Walk through any casino and you may get the feeling that you're at the U.N. It's not unusual to hear dialect from Italy, France, Greece, or Japan — cultures that are so different from one another in language, customs, and philosophy. But they all agree on one thing: it's good when the dealer breaks. Some come weekly, monthly, or yearly. Some only need to come just once.

Dan Hernon, an Army engineer from Atlanta, had never been to Atlantic City before. Stopping at Bally's, the first casino he saw, Dan felt lucky after reading his horoscope that day and decided to play a $1 progressive slot machine. About 90 minutes later, Dan Hernon won a cool $1 million! Prior to that grand finale, Dan went to a bingo game and won two jackpots, one for $500 and one for $750. I wonder if Dan bought any lottery tickets while he was in New Jersey?

Before the gambling referendum passed, someone suggested turning Atlantic City into a retirement community. In a strange way, the casinos that eventually came have provided a leisure activity for the elderly.

"This sure beats shuffle-board," said Sally as she tried to draw a third ace on a quarter poker machine. Sally and her husband, Phil, celebrated their 50th wedding anniversary with a weekend trip to Atlantic City six years ago. Sally and Phil now celebrate every Monday and Thursday at Trump Plaza. Sally went on to say, "All my aches and pains disappear when I'm here. See my husband walking toward us? I can tell he won just by the way he's walking."

How can you tell, Sally?

"He's not using his cane."

Felicia Campbell wrote a thesis on "Gambling Mythologies and Typologies." She states that gambling permits many people, especially the elderly, to "lose themselves in the action of the moment."

Day or night, the excitement knows no timetable, no season. An alarm clock in all of us rings as we drive nearer to the city. The casino's lights brighten up the skyline — red, blue, and green reflecting off the ocean. Our Boardwalk becomes a set for a Fellini movie: men in tuxedos and Nike sneakers, women in designer jeans and high heels, children with ice-cream cones and sandcastle dreams, people walking with a slice of pizza in one hand and a coin-bucket in the other.

The perfectly manicured casinos take a back seat to the majestic beauty of the Atlantic Ocean. Where else can you watch an ocean stretch into infinity one minute and make a $5 blackjack bet the next? Certainly not in Las Vegas!

Built in 1870, the Boardwalk still holds a mystery of beauty, tradition, charm, and romance. Beneath a star-bright sky, the setting is perfect for young love. Haunting melodies still echo from the days when Glenn Miller, The Dorsey Brothers, and Benny Goodman played the old Steel Pier. Music that sent a generation off to war, comes to shore with the evening tide, and only those with a sentimental ear can hear it. But tonight, everyone can hear the melodic calling of "lady luck." After all, money won is twice as sweet as money earned.

The high rollers of the sea come by yachts with cute names that must have some hidden meaning to them: Ace Of My Heart, My Lucky Lady, Soft 17, Seven Come Eleven, 777. Docking in the Marina, these sea travelers come equipped with swanky clothes, jewels, a bronze tan, cats and dogs, and most importantly, *money*. They come to help balance nature by relieving the ocean of its fish population. And to help keep the economy in balance they try to relieve the casinos of their money. We have all heard the fishermen's tale about the one that got away. But have you ever heard the casino floorman's tale?

"There's this high roller who we call Charlie the Tuna. Charlie loves to fish and play blackjack, but not necessarily in that order. On his last trip here he wasn't catching any fish, but he sure was catching some cards. He was up over $80,000 after two days and complained about his bad fishing luck, saying that if he didn't catch any fish tomorrow he would leave. He was fishing for blue marlin and going about 75 miles out. Now I know nothing about fishing. When you grow up in New York, fishing to me was driving over to Fulton's Fish Market every Friday afternoon. So, not wanting him to leave, at least not just yet, I told him to go 125 miles out to sea in a southwest direction. The following night he comes in with a smile on his face. He caught a thousand-pound marlin! In the days that followed he caught four marlins each weighing close to a thousand pounds! As he was signing a check over to the casino for $150,000 to cover his losses, he told the casino host he couldn't remember ever having so much fun. The casino host gave him a comp for dinner at the hotel's gourmet seafood restaurant. But 'Charlie' told her, 'Thanks but no thanks, you see I'm allergic to seafood!' "

Who among us can deny that ecstatic feeling we get when dealt a blackjack? Or the instant recognition as strangers gather around a bell-ringing slot machine. Or just the plain beauty that can be found in the game itself. A pair of dice, as if in slow motion, float effortlessly through the air, suspended in time, in space. Newton's theory proves to be true as the dice gently fall onto the green felt table.

Ever so gently, like Jack Nicklaus hitting a nine-iron, or a ballerina dancing the Nutcracker: ever so softly, the dice spin around and around. You hold your breath; all eyes watching, waiting. Then, from across the concert hall, a cheer crescendos into a roar. The applause begins; the critics have spoken; the show *will* continue.

Before the stickman can make the call, you already know you are a winner! For a moment in time you're somebody, like Joe Montana throwing the winning touchdown pass, or Meryl Streep winning the Oscar. You have arrived. The spotlight is yours. "WELCOME TO ATLANTIC CITY."

But how did this summer resort noted for saltwater taffy, Monopoly, and Miss America Pageants, suddenly become one of the biggest tourist attractions in the country? A city that 20 years ago was on the verge of financial ruin without a glimmer of hope. A summer resort that was once called "the champagne of the Jersey shore," turned into a bottle of sour wine. Tossed into the ocean, that bottle is floating back. And this time the label will read, Dom Perignon!

CHAPTER 2

Those Were The Days

Watergate, inflation, high unemployment, a 55-mph speed limit, rising oil prices. Muhammad Ali regained the heavyweight title by knocking out George Foreman. The Miami Dolphins won the Super Bowl. Babe Ruth's home-run record was broken by Hank Aaron. Bob Woodward and Carl Bernstein topped the nonfiction bestseller list with *All The President's Men*. Jack Benny, Dizzy Dean, Duke Ellington, Ed Sullivan, poet Anne Sexton, all made the obituary section of the New York Times. Stevie Wonder took home four Grammy Awards. The Sting won the Oscar.

If you remember any of those events, then welcome to the club. The year was 1974.

With inflation and interest rates topping out the year at twelve percent, most economists were yelling "fire." But one business seemed to thrive and showed no signs of slowing down. Illegal gambling was a healthy $23 billion-a-year business.

Have you ever wondered how the government comes up with these figures? Image the following scenario taking place at the White House:

SENATOR ODDS: Good morning gentlemen. Today we're going to investigate illegal gambling. I have a telephone number, which for the record, was given to me by my brother-in-law, which was given to him by his barber. It is my understanding that this number belongs to one of the biggest bookie operators on the East Coast. Senator Dimes, would you pass me the phone please.

MAN'S VOICE: Hello, Otto's barber shop.

SENATOR ODDS: Excuse me, I think I have the wrong number. I'm trying to reach a Mr. Point-Spread. Oh, that's you. Mr. Spread this is the United States Government calling from Washington, D.C. The point-spread on the Redskins game? Maybe some other time. The reason I'm calling is to find out how business is lately.

MAN'S VOICE: Is this Mark Russell?

SENATOR ODDS: Very funny. You may not be aware of the fact that the country is in a recession period and my constituents were wondering how it was affecting you? Oh really, you're up 24 percent from last year? I see you also make money selling wigs. Oh, *vigs,* could you please explain that?

That same year, the government sponsored a study on the economical and psychological effects of legalized gambling. The study concluded that gambling on state-run lotteries and off-track betting (OTB) proved to be unharmful to the average American family. The states' revenue from legalized gambling fell way below the government's expectations, and by all accounts, there was no significant cut into the profits of illegal gambling operations. The government thought that easing off on the imposed federal tax on winnings would perhaps make them more competitive. Have you ever heard of a bookie asking someone for their social security number? The old adage, "if you can't beat 'em, join 'em," was starting to prove itself true again.

U.S. News & World Report published the following statement from the government's study: "Gambling, whether it is legal or illegal, appears to provide an escape from the frustrated ambitions by offering the hope of a better life to people who otherwise have little expectation of improving their socioeconomic status. From this point of view, provision of a legal outlet can be construed as fulfilling a social need."

"Honey, take the kids on the Boardwalk for some ice cream. I'm going over to that craps table to fulfill my social need."

The government was finally learning something from the Al Capone and Bugsy Siegel schools of business: Legal, or illegal, gambling is big business. Bigger than U.S. Steel, to quote a line from the movie, The Godfather.

1974 Gambling Referendum Sevened Out

Like a weekend tourist caught up in the ocean's undertow, Atlantic City's "champagne bottle" was drifting further and further out to sea. The overwhelming problems of high unemployment, and the need to extend the tourist season, showed no signs of improving. Drowning in a financial sea of problems, the city was looking for someone to throw it a life preserver, preferably one shaped like a craps table. What it got instead was an inflatable tire that leaked all its air halfway to shore. On November 5th, the voters in New Jersey decisively rejected legalized statewide casino gambling by a 400,000 vote margin. Even though a study by the University of Michigan found that 88 million people — or 61 percent of the adult population in the United States — participated in some form of gambling, the New Jersey voters rejected the referendum.

Another important vote was taking place in Rush Springs, Oklahoma (pop. 1,381). The citizens decided to outlaw dancing in public.

Of the four anti-casino committees, the largest and most active was called Casinos-No Dice. The chairperson was Mercer County State Senator, Anne Martindell. Spending less than $20,000, and with support from clergymen, state legislators, and law-enforcement officials, the Casinos-No Dice coalition made a come-from-behind stretch-run to defeat the gambling referendum. Most political handicappers considered them to be the longshot because the pro-gambling forces had spent more than $500,000.

Many prominent and well-respected people joined the anti-casino campaign. Commissioner of baseball, Bowie Kuhn, was quoted as saying: "Casino gambling in New Jersey could lead to gambling on athletic events that would undermine public confidence in sports." Hey, Bowie, did you really think anyone would actually believe that!?

This ridiculous statement was made 15 years before Pete Rose was banned from baseball for gambling *illegally* on sporting events. Pete never had a problem with *legalized* gambling. In fact, when Pete Rose was playing for the Phillies, and living within a one-hour drive of Atlantic City, he never was seen gambling at any casino in town. Over 70 years ago, America's pastime was scarred with the fixing of the 1919 World Series, the infamous "Black Sox." That event took place 69 years before legalized gambling was introduced to Atlantic City.

Controversy would later arise when Mickey Mantle and Willie Mays accepted jobs as public consultants for two casinos. They were both threatened with a suspension from baseball and the Hall Of Fame. The "say hey kid" and Mickey were guilty of trying to make a living, and playing golf with casino high rollers. I guess it's all right for athletes to stand in front of a camera and argue over a can of beer: less filling, tastes great. I wonder what would happen if a beer company bought a casino?

Newark Mayor, Kenneth A. Gibson, in a New York Times article said: "The gambling proposal is dangerous, and will skyrocket law-enforcement problems if it is approved."

The New Jersey Council Of Churches ran an ad in the Atlantic City Press stating: "Casinos attract hustlers, loan sharks, con men, pimps, prostitutes, racketeers, drifters. Do you want this in your home state?''

The Atlantic City Christian Association expressed their feelings about gambling this way: "The Bible forbids gambling. Obey God's Commandments. Vote NO CASINO.''

How about bingo?

"The Bible doesn't mention bingo, my son.''

This ad also ran in the Atlantic City Press: "A Federal study on Gambling says, 'Compared to the cost of government, to say nothing of the potential social costs, the revenues that could be made by taxing or operating casinos in these states would be trivial.' ''

Listen up, guys. Atlantic City casinos, over a ten-year period, have paid $3.5 billion in federal, state, and local taxes. Hey boss, can I have a raise? Nothing big, just "trivial.''

The Casinos-No Dice campaign kept stressing to the voters that organized crime would invade the state if gambling were approved. William Lynch, chief of the Justice Department's organized crime and racketeering section said: "People in New Jersey talk about tight controls and state licensing, but the first ones to line up for a casino license will be those who've been running illegal gambling businesses.''

Ralph Salerno, former head of the New York City police department's racket squad, told Time Magazine: "I have no confidence in the screening process. I know of no jurisdiction where they can keep a mobster from owning a gin mill. Why should they be able to keep them out of Atlantic City?''

John Tompkin, a writer for Time, interviewed a former Mafia lieutenant who was living under police protection and an assumed name. The Mafia informant had this to say: "Your biggest gamblers are in the Northeast. It's the greatest thing in the world for the mob, and there's no way to keep 'em out. Who's going to be the pit bosses, the money handlers? Nobody but the mob has the money for casinos. Guys will come out of the woodwork down there lookin' like clergymen and askin' for a license."

Election day, November, 1974, and the vote wasn't even close. Las Vegas could rest easy.

The day after the referendum was defeated, everyone was taking credit for the "victory." Senator Martindell gave these reasons for the referendum's defeat:

1. The people knew it was not going to bring in the revenue it promised. (Fact: the revenues from casinos have surpassed all predictions. In 12 years of operating, casinos showed gaming revenues of $22.6 billion.)

2. It was not going to bring in the jobs it promised. (Fact: casinos have created over 50,000 jobs.)

Clergymen were claiming that the fear of God led the voters down the righteous path to a "no" vote. Law-enforcement officials said it was the fear of the God-*father!* But what really rubbed out the referendum was a single word: "statewide." Many people throughout the state had no religious or moral objections with legalized gambling, as long as the neon signs weren't in their backyards.

Even though Governor Byrne and other state legislators assured the public that casinos would only be allowed to operate in Atlantic City, that one word — "statewide," left room for doubt in the voter's mind. The Governor was quoted as saying: "I will veto any legislation extending operations of casinos to other communities. I will not turn New Jersey into Nevada by plunging into casino gambling on a wholestate basis."

Gloom and dismay covered Atlantic City the morning after the election. The city was in a state of depression, emotionally and financially. The Fat Lady sang, but no one was dancing. Mayor Bradway gave the local residents a locker-room pep talk: "Now is not the time to lay down and die. We will work together in an effort to make Atlantic City and Atlantic County what it should be."

The opposing team's locker-room was in full celebration. The biggest upset of the year was taking place. Mrs. Martindell, hosting a victory party at her Princeton home, said: "I thought it would be close, but I really did not think we would win." The constitutional amendment to permit casino gambling was overwhelmingly rejected by the voters. The score-board read: Pro-Casinos, 790,777; Casinos-No Dice 1,202,638. Mrs. Martindell went on to say: "The voters have seen through the flim-flam put out at the vast expense by the backers of the casino gambling and their shadowy allies. This is the end of the casino gambling issue in New Jersey, if not forever then at least for a decade."

You wouldn't want to bet on that?

A tropical, or rather a *topical* storm hit Atlantic City in 1974. Without rain or wind, the destruction was devastating to the heart and soul of the city. Comedians began using Atlantic City for a punch-line. Time Magazine quoted one comic as saying: "This town really swings. Every Friday night we shop till ten at the supermarket. Listen, the typical couple visiting Atlantic City these days is a very old lady... and her mother."

While the Casinos-No Dice coalition was celebrating, the pro-casino camp, having lost the first half, wasted no time and reorganized. A new approach was needed if they were to succeed in making Atlantic City the "Las Vegas" of the East.

Steven Perskie, who was recently appointed chairman of the Casino Control Commission, along with Senator Joseph McGahn and Assemblyman Howard Kupperman, rewrote the referendum language. The new referendum would state that casinos be allowed to operate *only* in Atlantic City. This would take the fear out of statewide gambling.

The idea of taxing the casinos and using the revenues to aid the senior citizens and handicapped would also be written into the new referendum. No referendum ever failed with a tax proposal to aid the elderly.

Knowing that the prospect of a state-owned operation turned many voters off, they left out the wording of ownership altogether. Because the state constitution prohibits the same issue from appearing on the ballot in successive election years, these new revisions would enable the proposal to get a second chance. All the Pro-Casino team needed now was a new quarterback.

CHAPTER 3

Mission Impossible

The time, 9 a.m.; the place, a telephone booth somewhere in San Francisco. A man, dressed in a neat pressed suit and smoking a cigarette, enters the phone booth.

"Good morning Mr. Weiner. Your mission, should you decide to accept it, is to help pass the gambling referendum in New Jersey. The code name of this mission will be called CRAC (Committee to Rebuild Atlantic City). As always, if you or any member of your CRAC force are caught or killed, Atlantic City will self-destruct in five seconds... uh, years. Good luck, Sanford. Oh, yeah... one more thing, smoking is bad for your health!"

Sanford Weiner, the ghostbuster of political consultants, arrived in Atlantic City in July, 1976, thus ending a year-long search for someone to head the CRAC campaign. Atlantic City was experiencing a heatwave with temperatures reaching the high 90s. Despite the heat and humidity, Weiner looked cool and confident. In his mid-40s, Weiner was the top man in his field. Having worked on 172 campaigns, he lost only 13. Of the 54 issues he packaged to the voters, all 54 were endorsed through referendum.

Working on the gambling referendum would be his biggest challenge to date. A referendum that only two years ago was defeated by a three-to-two margin. But Weiner was not the type of man who backed down from a challenge; he thrived on them. After packaging candidates and causes for 18 years, Weiner needed something to get his creative juices flowing.

His office on Atlantic Avenue could have been the set for an old Mickey Spillane movie. The building was old, but it had a peculiar charm about it. No hanging plants or wall-to-wall carpeting. The furniture was wood instead of wicker. Empty pizza boxes and coffee containers covered the desk. The stale smell of cigarette smoke hung in the air. An unlikely setting for a man on the verge of making history in New Jersey. An even more unlikely setting for a man making $2,300 a week.

The Saturday night regulars — Steve Perskie, Joseph McGahn, and Howard Kupperman — working side-by-side with Weiner, would spend many sleepless nights in this small narrow office. The mere presence of Weiner brought excitement back into the political establishment. Frank S. "Hap" Farley, former state senator and political boss, came out of retirement to lend his support to the committee. Mayor Joseph Lazarow gave not only his time and energy, but his creative input. It was Mr. Lazarow who chaired the Committee to Rebuild Atlantic City. Thousands of volunteers — the unsung heroes — were needed to make phone calls, address envelopes, and do the legwork necessary to win. A community composed of different ethnic and religious backgrounds joined hands and became one. The pride they felt for their city was overwhelming. They weren't ready to sit back and watch it die. The city still had its dignity. And the people, knowing that this would be their last chance, needed no pep-talk. Weiner, who now had his team assembled, rolled up his sleeves and went to work.

He started by re-decorating the office. Weiner papered the walls but not with flower prints or matching color schemes. He went for the avant-garde. Charts lined the walls: numbers on numbers, statistics, maps, and graphs. Like an artist facing a blank canvas, Weiner began to paint his masterpiece. Starting with a black and white sketch, the outline began to take on a form. A traditionalist, Weiner started as he always did, by studying the polls and surveys. Learning that 34 percent of the voters favored gambling and 31 percent opposed, Weiner went after the remaining 35 percent — the undecided. Recalled one volunteer worker, "Donald Trump might be 'the art of the deal,' but Sanford Weiner was the master of persuasion."

Weiner's psychology was to keep it simple, brief, and to the point. The official slogan for the campaign would be "Help Yourself." To avoid any misunderstanding about zoning, the words "Atlantic City Only" were printed beneath the slogan. "Casinos Yes" would be the tag line. Billboards, posters, and bumper stickers bearing the new campaign slogan could be seen on highways throughout the Garden State. With green as a background, the bold black and white lettering jumped out at the passing motorist.

Day by day, Weiner's painting began to materialize. Running out of green paint, Weiner would appeal to the patrons of the arts for financial support. With the new referendum leaving out all wording of ownership, the private sector would provide the funds needed to complete his masterpiece. Resorts International, having already spent $2.5 million for the Chalfonte-Haddon Hall Hotel, donated $200,000 to the CRAC committee. Many local motel owners made contributions of $10,000 or more.

The journalistic community questioned the integrity of the Atlantic City Press for its $45,000 contribution.

By Labor Day, nearly $1 million was raised. By Election Day, the total would exceed everyone's expectations. Weiner had enough green to paint the entire state.

As with all campaigns, this one would have its share of mudslinging. The Casinos-No Dice coalition, raising only $21,000, had to do something to deflate their opponents. When in doubt, talk about organized crime. After all, it worked in '74; why not in '76?

"The weight placed on law enforcement will be an unbearable one," said Clinton Pagano, superintendent of state police. Accusations that Resorts International had links to Meyer Lansky did little or nothing to sway the public. Resorts was accused of having connections with Howard Hughes and the CIA. Weiner accused the No Dice people of lowering themselves to McCarthy-like tactics. President Gerald Ford, campaigning in Atlantic City, said, "I personally oppose casino gambling." The President went on to say, "But I refuse to take a position on the referendum." Spoken like a true politician.

Four major counties in New Jersey got the full Weiner treatment: Essex, Bergen, Union, and Hudson counties crossed that very important undecided line. By late September, the Picasso of political consultants was putting the finishing touches on canvas. And that old bottle of sour wine, fermenting at sea, was returning home.

*"People who gave me their guts, their sweat
and their blood. In all my life I have never
seen so many dedicated people."*
Sanford Weiner
November 3, 1976

With sirens blasting, five police cars drove down Atlantic Avenue. Despite the cold November wind, a large crowd had gathered in front of the CRAC headquarters. A little girl asked her mother, "Who's coming, Mommy?" Her mother thought for a second then replied, "Santa Claus." The little girl studied her mother for a moment and said, "Do you believe in Santa Claus, Mommy?"

"I do today, sweetheart."

The sirens went silent as the police escort stopped in front of the waiting crowd. Emerging from the backseat of his car, Weiner was given a hero's welcome. Addressing the crowd, Weiner said, "My friends, this city is alive again tonight. The people of New Jersey finally responded to the need here. It's not a close victory. It's an outstanding victory." Praising Senator Joseph McGahn, and Assemblymen Howard Kupperman and Steve Perskie, Weiner went on to say, "It's party time in Atlantic City."

A sign posted on one of the roads leaving Atlantic City summed it up best. It read, "If Atlantic City doesn't get casino gambling, will the last person to leave the island please turn off the lights?"

Clean-up crews were already in Weiner's office getting it ready for the next tenant. Weiner's wallpaper was the first thing to go. It took seconds to tear down four months of work. Geoffrey Douglas, writer for New Jersey Monthly, got these afterthoughts from Weiner: "I wouldn't have gone near it two years ago. The voters weren't going to buy it the way it was written. They didn't go for the idea of casinos in their backyards."

In the Lone Ranger tradition, Weiner rode out of town 1976-style, in a jet. Somewhere, someplace, a candidate or a cause was waiting for him. Sanford Weiner gave Atlantic City a second chance, something most of us will never get in life. Atlantic City gave Sanford Weiner something that hopefully will last a lifetime — love. For in the midst of a hard-fought campaign, the old proverb "love conquers all" prevailed. Sanford Weiner left Atlantic City a married man.

It would have been ironic if the Weiners went to Paradise Island in the Bahamas on their honeymoon. A certain taxicab driver on that island would have loved to shake Weiner's hand. And here's why:

About six months before the November election, our friend the taxi driver picked up two Resorts executives at a golf course. His curiosity was aroused when he overheard their conversation about the possibility of Resorts International becoming the first casino to open in the soon-to-be gambling capital of the world. Buying a newspaper, the driver turned to the financial page, the racing form for the corporate world. Knowing nothing about handicapping stocks didn't faze him at all; he had gotten a tip right from the horse's mouth.

Resorts was selling for about $2 a share, the perfect price range for a $2 bettor. He bought 2,000 shares, leaving $100 in the bank, just in case. A few years later he sold 2,000 shares of Resorts International for $180 a share. Forget about price ratio, bullish and bearish, interest rates, the yen, and the Dow Jones average. Being in the right place at the right time... isn't that what life's all about?

CHAPTER 4

Pass Go
And Collect $$$

Atlantic City's new Monopoly board would read, "Pass Pacific Avenue" and buy everything in sight. Eighteen months before the first roll of the dice, land speculators looking for action came East. Property worth $70,000 was now selling for seven *hundred* thousand dollars! Before the gambling referendum was passed, many local motel owners were willing to sell out for less than a million dollars. The new asking price — $5 million and up... and it was considered a *bargain*.

For 15 years, Madame Lida worked the Atlantic City Boardwalk. Sitting in a small booth she would read your palm for a dollar. Teenagers with Rolling Stones tee-shirts and summer jobs would test her skills. Their innocent eyes would open wide with amazement as predictions of wealth and happiness filled the tiny booth. Teenage girls would someday marry and have two children, a boy and a girl. Every teenage boy was guaranteed a passing grade in algebra and a new Corvette.

In the summer of '76, Madame Lida gave Newsweek magazine some free and very accurate predictions. She read Atlantic City's palm as if it were her own. "There will be packed beaches and gleaming new high-rises. Long black limousines will snake through crowded streets alongside stylish mopeds." Maybe she meant jitneys instead of mopeds. Madame Lida continued, "But as for me, I don't see a whole lot. The truth is, I won't be around, kid. This city will be full of sleek, sophisticated outsiders with lots of style."

Newsweek found another fortune teller in Reese Palley, the purveyor of crystal. Looking into his crystal ball, Palley said, "This is a magic city, man, total magic. There is no place else in America to put a dollar where it will get a sure return quicker." Palley followed his own advice and bought the 75-year-old Marlborough-Blenheim Hotel located at Park Place and the Boardwalk. In 1977, Bally Manufacturing Corp. leased the property for $850,000 a year, giving Reese Palley's crystal ball a new "lease" on life. Two years later Bally purchased the property.

Legalized gambling was coming out of the closet and the American public liked what it saw. Other states were now considering legalized gambling as an alternative to their economic woes. New York's Governor Hugh Carey and Mayor Abe Beame stated publicly that legalized gambling might be good for New York State. New Hampshire and Connecticut started presenting the idea of casinos to the people.

Florida, remembering the good ol' days when illegal casinos prospered in the Miami Beach area, was now appraising the idea of *legal* casino gambling. A local resident said: "People want oranges on slot machines, not trees." A local goverment official had these thoughts: "People come here on package deals. Then they fly over to the Bahamas for the day and blow $1,000 gambling. Why not keep that money in the States?"

Gambling around the world was becoming an important growth industry. The geographical lure of Lady Luck is worldwide, from the peasant farmer in Europe to the successful industrialist in Japan.

With gambling in Atlantic City still 18 months away, the invasion was in full swing. Hitting the beaches, the "risk-takers" came equipped with heavy artillery: money, blank checks, and big credit lines.

Opportunity wasn't knocking on Atlantic City's door, it was kicking it down! Resorts International purchased the Chalfonte-Haddon Hall Hotel for $5.2 million five months *before* the gambling referendum was passed! I can safely say that this had to be the biggest "pass-line" bet in gambling history! That check would snowball into an avalanche, although no one, even the people at Resorts, knew what kind of snow machine they were sitting on.

The Chalfonte-Haddon Hall Hotel, an Atlantic City landmark, had fallen victim to Father Time. Like an aging beauty queen, clinging to a scrapbook of memories, the glamor had faded. There was a time when grace and elegance seemed never-ending. Like youth and love, winter comes all too soon for those who watch the clock. Though time may wrinkle the smoothest of skin, and grey the darkest of hair, that "fountain of youth" can be found in all of us, if we look hard enough.

Like eyes gazing out into the Atlantic, the hotel's windows looked tired. Maybe the endless years of fighting off storms had taken its toll. How many ships lost at sea have used these lamp-bright windows as a guide to bring them safely home? A lighthouse for the lost and weary. If walls could talk they would tell us tales about American presidents sipping cognac and coffee with foreign royalty. Or secret meetings hosted by Al Capone.

Somewhere in this aging hotel, a theater sits in darkness. The spotlight no longer shines. The curtain no longer rises. Once a cathedral for the world's greatest opera singers. The melodies of Wagner and Puccini no longer crescendo. The steady rhythm of a carpenter's hammer breaks the cold silence. But high in the balcony, in the last row, a voice can be heard saying, "bravo!" The Chalfonte-Haddon Hall, though tired and grey, has found the fountain of youth.

> *...old things are passed away, behold, all things are become new.*
>
> II Corinthians 5:17.

In October 1976, Resorts made out a non-refundable check for $200,000 as a deposit on a 56-acre ocean-front tract. Resorts intended to use 17 acres to build a 1,000-room hotel at a cost in excess of $75 million. Resorts hired John Calvin Portman Jr., the Toscanini of the architectural world. And like the "maestro" of old, Portman designs were said to be "radical" and "spectacular." His designs were original, inspirational, and admired worldwide. He wanted his work to become a symbol of Atlantic City's rebirth. Before lifting a pencil, Portman would take easy strolls along the Boardwalk to capture the "spirit" of Atlantic City. As he put it: "I am in a period of total research."

All eyes and ears were on Atlantic City now. Every move was photographed, every word found a reporter eager to listen. The enthusiasm felt on North Carolina Avenue was contagious. Along the Boardwalk, merchants who were tired of long winters and slow summers started painting their storefronts. The Paul Reveres of Atlantic City weren't on horseback. They were the locals walking down the street and passing the word, "The casinos are coming, the casinos are coming."

Resorts International, originally a small paint company based in North Miami, Florida, would soon put Atlantic City back on the map. When the late John Crosby purchased the company in 1958, it was called Mary Carter Paint. In 1960, his son, James, became the company's chairman. I.G. "Jack" Davis, a Harvard-educated businessman and jogging advocate, was president of the company. The two men reached a decision: The color of money doesn't come in a gallon can of latex, it comes from a guy willing to bet $50,000 a hand. The "painting" on the wall said, sell.

In May 1968, Crosby sold Mary Carter Paint for $9.9 million. They changed the company's name to Resorts International. Before the money had a chance to dry, they bought their first casino, on Paradise Island in the Bahamas.

In this "high gloss" business of gambling, timing and luck is a marriage made in financial heaven. Show me a company that doesn't take a risk, and I'll show you a bore. Here's a company that came to Atlantic City in 1976, shortly after the referendum was voted down. They came to town to play only one hand — winner take all. The climate in Jersey was still anti-gambling.

Resorts was playing blackjack and the state was dealing a 12-deck game. They put their money down on a 50-year-old hotel and then waited to play out the hand. Some said they were crazy. But on opening night eve, these two "wild and crazy guys," though unknown to them, were on the brink of making gambling history.

Atlantic City would rise up from the ashes and send a smoke signal west. Somewhere over the Nevada desert, a cloud of smoke appeared high in the sky. The letters were clear for all to read: "Look out Nevada, you're not the only game in town!"

But unlike the "old days" in Las Vegas, when men like Moe Sedway, Frank Costello, and Benjamin "Bugsy" Siegel ruled the casino world, Atlantic City would open with a cleaner image, and, in the process, pave the way for other legitimate companies and individuals to take part in this growing industry. Resorts would also put to rest that old joke:

"Anything that's fun is either illegal, immoral, or fattening." Gambling in New Jersey would no longer be illegal or immoral. And, the Sweet Shop in Resorts advertised *diet* ice cream.

CHAPTER 5

Let The Games Begin

A roulette wheel spins in perfect rhythm. The players around the table are composing, by number. Dealers with perfect pitch arrange each note.

"No more bets," echoes over the table. All eyes follow the bouncing ball. No one blinks as the ball jumps in and out of numbered pockets, like fingers on a piano playing scales and arpeggios, building to that grand finale.

Just as that final chord approaches, someone decides to add one more note. "No bet," said the dealer. The harmony is broken, misunderstood. A dispute becomes unavoidable. The player raises his voice. People walking past the game stop. The dealer remains cool as he explains the rules to the player.

Over at a craps table, the action is slow moving, even though five people are playing. The dealers are making sure each payoff is correct. A player chewing on a cigar throws a chip toward the stickman, "press my hard eight." A lady dressed stylishly and looking confused asks the stickman, "what's the payoff on that?" The stickman, in a very courteous voice answers the lady's question. A player "buys" the ten. Again the lady's curiosity becomes aroused. But this time she directs her question to one of the dealers.

At a blackjack table, the dealer draws a fifth card for a total of 21. After seeing his cards picked up, a man sitting on first base informs the dealer, in no uncertain terms, that he too had 21. The dealer calls his supervisor over and is instructed to remove the cards from the discard rack and "back deal" the hand. The results were unchanged. The dealer did in fact have a five-card total of 21, and the player had a six-card total of 20.

"See, you lose," said the young nervous dealer. The first-base player would hear no more. Standing up and looking straight into the dealer's eyes he said, "Never, never, say the word *lose* to a player." Then, looking into the eyes of the other players, he continued, "And don't ever forget that."

What is this, a dealer's nightmare? A pit boss' idea of a bad joke? Dealer burn-out? No, this was a test. The roulette dealer, craps dealer, and stickman passed. The blackjack dealer would stay after school.

Who, disguised as a blackjack player, faster than a dealer eating a 20-minute meal, able to count tall stacks of chips at a single bound — no, it's not Superman, but you're getting warm. It's a gaming supervisor! And that wasn't Lois Lane at the craps table. In real life, she's a shift boss. The roulette player was a pit boss.

With opening day a little over a week away, Resorts was having a test run. Most of the dealers have never dealt outside the classroom. And in this business there's no summer school. These casino virgins would soon learn that it's not all glitter and glamour behind the tables! Said one 25-year casino veteran, "If you're looking for fun, join the Marines."

Resorts invited off-duty hotel employees, their families and friends for a few nights of "fake money" gambling. A dress rehearsal before opening night. Over 2,500 employees, (400 of them dealers) were hired on a full-time basis. Most of them had never been in a casino before. Many were moonlighting from their present jobs: School teachers, nurses, bank clerks, housewives, auto salesmen, mechanics — all tired of the nine-to-five rat race.

Hoping to meet their "prince charming," sweet young girls with beautiful smiles and perfect legs applied for cocktail-waitress positions. "Give 'em a month," said a Vegas transplant, "and they won't be so sweet and naive anymore. This ain't no place for a cheerleader."

"I've been a wardrobe mistress for a long time," said Marie as she made another adjustment on the newly arrived cocktail outfits. "The first thing I give my girls is the phone number of a good chiropractor. High heels and a tray full of drinks don't mix."

Casino Manager Walter I. Rogers, and Hotel President Anthony M. Rey observed these fake money nights and felt confident that the new dealers could handle opening night without any problems. Six dealers, having the night off, were playing baccarat. As Mr. Rogers walked into the pit, a security guard recognizing him asked if the players could keep the money if they won? "Sure they can," Mr. Rogers said. "It has no value."

Most of the personnel hired to work in the "pits" came from Nevada. A pit boss was overheard saying, "Do you realize I've been in this business longer than the average

age of the kids they have dealing here?" After years of working with experienced dealers, these "old timers" showed little patience for rookies.

"You need people with experience to oversee the inexperienced," said a hotel executive. The relaxed atmosphere on the "fake money" nights inspired a pit boss to say: "Tonight it's fun and games. The real test will come when the *real* money is played. Did you ever look into a player's eyes after he dropped $100,000? It's like looking into the barrel of a shotgun. A loaded shotgun. Only the strong survive in this business."

For some veterans of the casino world it was a homecoming. "I was born and raised about three blocks from here," said another casino executive. "I went to Nevada in 1948 and never came back. After 30 years in this business I needed something new, a challenge. I never opened a casino before. I feel like a Broadway producer waiting for the opening-night curtain call."

What do you think the reviews will say? "Resorts International, the hottest ticket in town."

At the end of the final practice day, most of the 400 dealers had the honor of hearing one more pep-talk. A man resembling General Patton gave these final instructions to the troops: "Don't say, 'You look tired!' Don't say, 'Yeah' or 'OK', all right? Don't use vulgar language." Standing in the back of the room, a dealer raised her hand. "But what if someone curses at me?" she asked. Without the slightest bit of hesitation the "general" said, "Let them. That means they're losing."

The bartenders and waitresses were given these final instructions: "When serving beer, soda, or champagne, don't leave any empty bottles in the casino. Someone playing a slot machine might get mad and hit it with an empty bottle.''

In the early morning hours, the casino was almost empty. Except for the cleaning crew, all was quiet, like the calm before the storm. The 84 gaming tables and 893 slot machines were all in place. The new chips were sleeping peacefully in their new home.

Resorts wanted to open on May 26, 1978. Only one thing was missing — a license. The law required that all applicants fill out an 83-page form. The Casino Control Commission wanted to know the complete personal and business background of all those applying for a gambling license. The only problem was that the investigations lasted six to nine months. Having submitted an application on December 22, 1977, Resorts still was waiting for the CCC's decision.

Adding more ''red tape'' to the delay was the Division of Gaming Enforcement. Every employee had to be finger-printed and photographed. The DGE had to process every potential applicant's form. The paperwork was staggering and the under-staffed DGE was way behind schedule. Said one investor watching from the sidelines, ''By the time these agencies make up their minds, casinos will open in Miami, New York, and the Poconos.''

On May 25th, the Casino Control Commission decided to issue Resorts a temporary permit. The casino could now open its doors to the public. Since mid-winter, Resorts had been meeting the staff payroll without knowing when they could open for business. ''But now,'' said chairman James Crosby, ''we'll make money. Oh, we'll make money all right.'' History was only 24 hours away.

*"My father always told me,
never to bet on anything
but Notre Dame and the Yankees
but for anyone not willing
to take my father's advice,
I now declare this casino open."*
         Governor Brenden Byrne, May 26, 1978

The New York Times called it "Woodstock by the Sea." Thousands of people, some curious, and others not wanting to miss the opening day ceremonies, drove down to Atlantic City. Sitting on the podium waiting for the Governor is Mayor Joseph Lazarow, Frank Farley, Senator Joseph McGahn, Assemblyman Howard Kupperman, and Jack Davis, President of Resorts International. Steve Perskie is waiting for the Governor's helicopter at Bader Field. Governor Byrne's advance man, Russell Corby, has been running around the Boardwalk since six a.m., and his patience is running thin. High school bands, clowns, and majorettes are waiting for their cue. To put it mildly, it was bedlam.

For those inside Resorts, it was another story. Like a fighter waiting for the first-round bell to ring, the dealers stared across the empty floor in silence. Donald Borino stood behind his blackjack table waiting, and wondering what this day would bring. He graduated from dealer's school only four days earlier. He said he wasn't nervous, only excited. "A lot of us here were out of work before Resorts came to town."

Rumors were flying around the casino. "There's a line of people stretching for miles waiting to get in," a security guard announced. A gaming supervisor looking at a young dealer said, "Are you all right?" "I guess so," said the dealer, trying to hide the nervousness in his voice. Pausing for a moment, he then said, "I think I have to go to the bathroom." The gaming supervisor walked over to the dealer. He put his arm on the dealer's shoulder, the way a father might do just before telling his son the "facts of life." In a fatherly voice the supervisor said, "Kid, you're a dealer now. And dealers only go to the bathroom on their breaks. Hold it, you'll be fine."

Another supervisor smiled and talked to himself as he walked around the casino. "So this is what a new casino looks and smells like? The carpet has no cigarette burns in it. And it smells like a florist shop."

Outside, the crowd was getting impatient. The Governor was behind schedule. Television stations sent camera crews down to give the rest of the nation a chance to see this historic day. Waiting is nothing new for a newspaper reporter. Drinking coffee, they threw peanuts to the pigeons to pass the time. Clowns were passing out buttons that said: "You Can Bet Atlantic City Loves You."

Policemen moved the crowd so that the Governor's car, a green convertible, could pass. Above the cheering and applause, the song, "Happy Days Are Here Again" could be heard. The same song that once ended the Depression era would now bring in a new era. Only this time it would be anything but depressing.

Those who planned this event were concerned about the weather. High above the ocean, dark clouds threatened rain. As the Governor waved to the crowd, the clouds moved farther and farther out to sea. The sun, like a stage spotlight, shined on everyone. Perhaps it was a coincidence. Or was it a sign of things to come?

The Governor began his speech: "I use the term Queen of Resorts, not King of Resorts, because queen imparts a sense of dignity and gentleness, and Atlantic City meets that description." The thousand-plus crowd rose to their feet and applauded. The Governor held his hands high to quiet the crowd. The only sound that could be heard was the clicking of cameras as photographers, jockeying for position, took aim.

Reporters held tape recorders high waiting for the Governor to continue. Like a seasoned politician, after years of endless dinner speeches, the Governor paused. His timing was perfect, absolute; the punch line was coming. His voice changed as he spoke. He would settle this issue once and for all.

> *"I've said it before and I will repeat it again to organized crime: Keep your filthy hands off Atlantic City! Keep the hell out of our state."*

If a building could smile, then the 50-year-old Haddon-Hall had a grin on its face a mile long. The hotel opened its arms to the thousands of visitors who came to praise Resorts, although most came to conquer!

On May 26, 1978, gambling rolled into New Jersey. The dealers watched, almost in fear, as people ran into the casino. "It looked like a cattle stampede," said one dealer. A pit boss watched in amazement as people surged into the casino, "It looks like 'Let's Make A Deal.'"

The first bet was made by singer Steve Lawrence, who with his wife, Eydie Gorme, were appearing in Resorts' Superstar Theater. Steve went to the craps table and bet ten dollars on the pass-line. He rolled a five. But this story would have no Hollywood ending. For on the very next roll, Steve rolled a seven.

Governor Byrne walked through Resorts later that afternoon. Seeing the massive crowds, the Governor said, "This will be the kick-off for a new revival." People waited in line for over two hours just to get inside to be *revived*. Inside, there were lines everywhere. People waited to get change. Standing four-deep at the blackjack tables, players waited for someone to "tap out" so they could play.

Some people came to make a killing, and others came to kill time. "It rained quarters," said Max Kleiman from Baltimore. Max and his wife, Hilda, were here on a convention. They stopped by Resorts just to "kill time." Max put five quarters into a machine and walked off with $125. The machine was set to only pay out only $50 in coins. The slot attendants were so busy paying out jackpots, that Max had to wait 45 minutes for his cash. But alas, Max never got to even hold the money. "He'll never see this money," Mrs. Kleiman said as she put the money in her purse. "This is not going back to the casino."

Said another player, "I can't get my husband to sit at my mother's house for 20 minutes. But he's been sitting at the blackjack table for 15 hours." Her husband answered, "I can't make $3,100 at your mother's house!"

A man playing roulette hugged his wife, "Honey, look, $350. I bet $10 on our wedding date, 24." The man's wife should have been happy, but she wasn't. "The 24th?" she said in a loud sarcastic voice. "We were married on the 21st. You married your *first* wife on the 24th." As she turned to walk away, her husband grabbed her arm. "Here's $300, go buy yourself a new dress."

While the action inside was hot and heavy, action of another kind took place outside. Penthouse magazine's "Pet of the Year," and Miss Atlantic City were participating in a media event. As lifeguards helped the two bikini-clad women into lifeboats, a crowd of men standing along the Boardwalk watched. One man asked, "Which one is from Penthouse?" The man standing next to him said, "I don't know. I can't tell with their clothes on."

One of the hotel's entertainers walked outside to get some fresh air. Someone waiting in line asked, "What's going on inside?" The entertainer shook his head saying, "Man, it's nuts in there. I heard people saying, 'Oh, God, give me a six.' If God could get a six, don't you think He'd be in there at a table, too?"

Bravo, Boardwalk, Bravo! No this wasn't a chant going on outside. This was also opening night for the hotel's production show called Bravo Boardwalk. Dancers, after days and nights of endless rehearsals, showed no sign of fatigue. Sore legs kicked high into the air in unison. Swollen ankles and shattered knees hit the hardwood stage. Twisting, turning... their perfectly tuned bodies moved gracefully. Yesterday they were strangers. Tonight they're a family — a chorus line. Egos and street clothes wait patiently in the dressing room. Later, alterations will be made. Needle and thread in one hand, tea and sympathy in the other.

Experience can only speak to those willing to listen. Those who hear, pace themselves. Save something for tomorrow night. Opening nights, closing nights, extended runs, smile, lose weight, kick higher, faster, spin, turn, do it again, Broadway, Vegas, Atlantic City.

Chorus girls travel light: make-up kit, character shoes, liniment for sore limbs, a friend's phone number for the a.m.

A dancer's best friend can be found in a dance studio. The mirror won't lie, and the "barre" supports the weak. Lights, camera, action, a life of glamour and a dozen roses from a handsome prince? Alice in Wonderland? Cinderella in glass slippers?

Hardly. From behind the spotlight, it's a world where youth and dreams melt quickly under the stage lights. In lavish costumes and layered make-up, they dance long into the night. Tomorrow, there will be last-minute changes, new routines. Rumors and liniment bottles will pass down the line. Will the show continue? Are they cutting my number? Will a younger girl replace me? Is it worth it?

Resorts appeared to be heading for a record-breaking $3 million weekend, despite the fact that ten blackjack tables were closed, and there was a shortage of change-persons. The CCC was still investigating the backgrounds of potential employees.

The statement, "Time is money," was never so true. A blackjack table on the Vegas Strip takes in about $425,000 a year, or about $35,000 per month. With ten tables down, Resorts was losing $350,000 a month. This figure is actually low if we were to take into account the large crowds that came to Resorts that opening weekend, not to mention the high rollers from the Northeast who couldn't get a seat at a table.

"I've been driving a cab waiting for the CCC to clear my dealer's license," said a waiting dealer. "You could get a gun permit faster.'' As the long holiday weekend progressed, so did the crowds. The waiting lines showed no signs of thinning down. The casino's purse got fatter and fatter.

The aisles by the slot machines looked like Times Square on New Year's Eve. If a slot machine broke down, there was only one way to get there — climb on top. ''I felt like a high-wire act in the circus,'' said one attendant. ''I had to climb on top of the machines and cat-walk over to the defective machine. Then, once I got there, I had to fight my way down.''

The action at the craps tables was nonstop. ''I've never seen so many parlay bettors in my life,'' said a craps dealer. ''Press, press, that's all I heard. I thought I was working in a Chinese Laundromat. Players wanted to walk out of here with a certificate of ownership.''

Slot bells rang. Dice clicked as they hit the wall. The shuffling of cards echoed down the aisles. Like the overture before a Broadway show, these melodies signaled a winner. The ''standing room only'' crowds tested their skills against the casino's law of probability. Silver turned to gold; gold to platinum. Atlantic City would become a speculator's dream and a prospector's domain. The gold rush was on. The news spread worldwide. Atlantic City would be a ghost town no more.

Resorts wanted to be the biggest casino in the world. There were only two things standing in its way: the MGM Grand in Vegas (now Bally's), and the temporary north wall in Resorts. One would fall victim to a sledge hammer; the other to a tragic fire. By mid-June, Resorts would add 500 more slot machines, 33 blackjack tables, four craps tables — and for all you carnival-type players — another Big Six wheel.

Resorts set a new worldwide record for gambling revenues. The casino's average daily win was over $750,000. By June of the first year, its total win was a staggering $62.8 million. The MGM Grand was considered casino King when they reported a gross win of $84 million, for the entire *year*! The oasis in the Nevada desert would no longer quench the kingdom's thirst. The King will no longer rule. Those disciples of fate who flirt with luck have been seduced to come East. The King reigns no more. Long live the Queen!

When the dust finally settled, Resorts went into the record books as the all-time high money-maker in the casino industry. On an average day, 80,000 people walked through the casino. Resorts won over $200 million that first year.

This aging resort town by the sea would no longer be a joke-writer's punch line. Atlantic City, like Carnegie Hall, became the stage to play. And players from everywhere stood waiting in the wings: Caesars, Bally's, TropWorld, Harrah's, Donald Trump, Del Webb, and Steve Wynn.

The older, established casinos moved cautiously. Their hearts were in Nevada; their future was in Atlantic City. The casino industry, as they knew it, was about to change, forever!

CHAPTER 6

Monopoly, Anyone?

Sometimes opportunity is simply a matter of being in the right place at the right time! Atlantic City, the Great Depression, and Charles B. Darrow, would prove this statement true. Unemployed and bored, Darrow invented the real estate board game, Monopoly. Parker Brothers acquired the rights to the game in 1935. Monopoly made Atlantic City famous and the Parker Brothers rich. Kitchen tables around the world would serve family and friends wheeling and dealing their way to fame and fortune. The object of the game is to become the wealthiest player through buying, renting, and selling property.

In the late '70s, the objective was the same, only this time the playing board would be slightly larger — nearly a mile wide, and over five miles long. But one thing would remain the same. A toss of the dice could either make you, or break you!

Atlantic City's first Monopoly player was a Quaker farmer. Thomas Budd, while walking along the beach in 1695, saw this sign:

For Sale

Beautiful beachfront property, ocean view.
Four cents an acre. Price negotiable.

In the late 1970s, "negotiators" came with pockets full of miracles and left with suitcases full of cash! Who were these high-stakes players and where did they come from? Those gurus who preach the "nothing down" sermon, came with nothing and left with nothing! This was strictly a cash and carry game.

Corporations from Vegas, New York, Japan, and Chicago came to play. Entrepreneurs were falling out of the sky and landing on the beach without parachutes! Atlantic City was becoming a year-round resort and everyone wanted a season! Casinos and Mother Nature would change the financial climate in Atlantic City. It was raining acquisitions and everyone was getting wet!

How do you parlay $12,000 into a billion-dollar casino empire? Sell a lot of hot dogs! Clifford and Stuart Perlman turned a little hot dog stand in Florida into a fast-food chain called Lum's. Zillions of hot dogs later, the Perlmans bought Caesars Palace in Las Vegas. In the late '70s, the Perlmans took over Howard Johnson's on the Boardwalk. "We're back to where we started from," said Stuart Perlman. "Over 30 years ago, my brother and I operated a beach chair concession. Only now we're on the other side of the Boardwalk."

Spending over $100 million on renovations, they transformed the Howard Johnson's Regency Motor Hotel into Caesars Boardwalk Regency — A Palace for the East-Coast gambler. The Perlmans weren't interested in Ho-

Jo's 28 flavors. Only one flavor whetted their appetites — *mint green*! Their 48,630 square-foot "ice cream parlor" would have 95 table games and 1,431 slot machines as an appetizer.

Caesars would open at the best of times and the worst of times: June 26, 1979, the beginning of summer, sunny days and warm summer nights. But an unforeseen villain was disrupting the cycle.

OPEC, a third-world cartel, was turning America into one big gas line. Pennsylvania, New Jersey, Delaware, and New York all adopted gasoline rationing. Fuel was in short supply. Casinos weren't the only ones with table minimums. New Jersey Governor Byrne ordered an odd-even system, and a $5 and $7 minimum purchase requirement.

Would people living over 100 miles away use their precious fuel for a day-trip to Atlantic City? Would OPEC destroy Atlantic City's day in the sun? Would OPEC conquer Caesar? Is the Pope Methodist? Of course not!

Thousands lined up on the Boardwalk waiting to hail Caesar. The crowd was so large that Caesars officials decided to only let 2,500 people in at a time. "We didn't want the casino to become overcrowded," said an official. "Gas lines and now casino lines," said one eager gambler. "But do you know what the sweetest line of all is? The coin-redemption line!"

J. Terrence Lanni, chairman of the Boardwalk Regency, watched the crowds filter into the casino. Resorts would no longer be the only game in town. Talking to Daniel Heneghan from the Atlantic City Press, Lanni said: "I first came here in 1977 when this was a desolated city. It's just amazing to see what has happened here in the last year and a half and we are all proud to be a part of it.''

Caesars in Atlantic City would take in $91.3 million that year with a profit of $16 million. That total would surpass the combined profits of their casinos in Vegas and Tahoe. Resorts and Caesars reported a total win of $324.2 million in 1979. They were taking a big bite out of Nevada's gambling pie.

''There is a tremendous market which has barely been tapped,'' said Philip Wechsler from Resorts. While Resorts and Caesars were busy ''tapping,'' the state was busy collecting. In 1979, the state collected $34.4 million in taxes from casino gambling. And over 11,000 casino-related jobs were created. The state received a special bonus of $319,392 from Resorts. It seems that their slot machines took in too much money during the summer of '78. I wonder if Resorts paid off the fine in nickels and quarters?

Card-counters were also taking in too much money according to the casinos. A 13-day test period took effect on December 1, 1979. The CCC wanted the casinos to experiment with a new ruling. If a player more than doubled their previous bet the dealer could reshuffle. This ''scientific'' test drew hundreds of card-counters back to the lab in the interest of science! According to ''scientists'' at Resorts and Caesars, the experiment cost them $1.4 million!

Slot machines took in too much money. Card-counters won over $111,000 a day. Property owners became instant multi-millionaires. Buildings were falling. Buildings were rising. Real estate lawyers hit the lottery jackpot. Accountants couldn't add fast enough. Construction sites stretched from one end of the Boardwalk to the other. Atlantic City was starting to look like the Promised Land.

Deals were made quickly. Hesitation was costly. Property selling for $6 million Monday was a bargain at $6.2 million Tuesday.

The race to acquire property left many standing at the starting gate. Corporations had a ten-length lead over the field. They were the house *and* the player, the bank and the banker, the oddsmakers. But a long-shot was making a stretch-run down the boardwalk. He was young and ambitious — a thoroughbred with confidence and a winner's-circle smile. The casino business was in his blood and veins. Atlantic City would embrace his style and make him a star — a very *rich* star!

It's a bright sunny afternoon in June. Resorts has been open for two weeks according to the calendar, and $4 million according to the accountants. A man looking like a nickel slot player dressed in sandals and a T-shirt stands gazing into the casino, three-deep at the tables with slot machines going non-stop. His eyes opened wide, like a tourist seeing the Statue of Liberty for the first time. He knew immediately that this truly was the land of opportunity. Later, he would tell his friends, "I saw more people betting more money than I'd ever seen in my life."

Walking down the Boardwalk he stopped at the Strand Motel. Twenty-five minutes and $8.5 million later, he owned it. Manny Solomon would lock the doors for the last time. Atlantic City, the Queen of Resorts, was being romanced by a knight in shining armor. The prince of the city has arrived. "Steve Wynn, welcome to Atlantic City."

Steve (The Mirage) Wynn, would give Atlantic City what the corporate-run casinos couldn't: a touch of class! "High play. That's what I love about this business," said Wynn. "Win or lose, I love to gamble high."

Most of us spend a lifetime chasing a dream. A race against time, where years and months flash by like minutes. Without prophecy or fulfillment we hold on to every dream. And when hope no longer sustains us, and payment for borrowed time is overdue, we fight the odds. In 1967, with $35,000 in borrowed cash, Wynn started chasing his dream. Three thousand miles later, the finish line was in sight. Like a marathon runner, Wynn got his second wind in Atlantic City!

His Boardwalk casino would become Atlantic City's wake-up call. It was rise and shine for the illusionist who cat naps, and for the Rip Van Winkles of the casino industry. The Golden Nugget was Atlantic City's 24-carat centerpiece. For Wynn, the search was over; the gold mine was found. Finding it was easy; getting here wasn't!

"I learned a good lesson early in life," said Wynn. "If you want to make money in the casino business... own one!"

Being long on ambition and short on cash doesn't guarantee a passing grade. Fifteen million in cash doesn't cover tuition fees in this business. Institutional investors were reluctant to finance casinos, but Wynn's aggressiveness would soon change their "old-school" way of thinking. "Steve can sell himself like no one else," said John Kissick, managing director for the former Drexel Burnham Lambert. Wynn needed $160 million to build the Golden Nugget in Atlantic City. Drexel would be the goose that laid the golden egg!

Charisma, charm, sophistication, and knowing how to mix it up with the high rollers, Wynn not only wrote the book — he designed the cover! From the Ivy Leaguers in Brook Brothers suits on Wall Street, to the craps shooter from the Bronx, Wynn spoke their language, knew their psyche. A smile, a handshake, and a few encouraging words from the master of human nature. Knowing how to make a loser feel like a winner, and an atheist a believer. Hope, in a casino, isn't the exit sign, it's the welcome mat!

The Golden Nugget towered over the Boardwalk — Atlantic City's Parthenon, a temple for the East Coast high roller. God created Man, Wynn created excitement! While others were building casinos, Wynn built an *attraction*! Opening in December 1980, the gold and white building brightened up the shore line.

The gambling industry was entering the technological age. Over the years, casinos fell victim to the corporate way: depersonalization, hierarchical structures, and above all... a lust for money-making. Gamblers became numbers fed into computers: zip codes, birth dates, player ratings, bank accounts, economic status, and demographic numbers. Technology may be cost-efficient and error-proof, but to the casinos, it helped forge profit at any cost. Wynn dared to be different; he took a giant step backwards, to the good old days.

The personal touch was missing in the Atlantic City casinos until Wynn's arrival. Wynn would become the modern-day version of Benny Binion, the legendary owner of the Horseshoe in Vegas. Like Binion, Wynn would walk through his casino shaking hands and greeting the customers, making them feel like royalty! And it goes beyond making simple comps. Just ask Sir Joey C. from Brooklyn:

"Listen, I remember hangin' out in a little neighborhood bar. As soon as I walked in the joint, the bartender, without asking, would pour me a Cutty and water. Made me feel important. I always left the guy a saw-buck. Two years later the bartender buys the joint."

What's that got to do with Steve Wynn?

"I'm gettin' to that, be patient. I'm leaning over the craps table and I hear someone say, 'How are you Mr. C?' I turn around and it's him, Steve Wynn. Get it?"

No.

"Steve is like that bartender. See this $1,000 pass-line bet? That goes into Steve's cup. Hey, the guy's got class. He kissed my wife's hand."

Wynn understood high rollers, after all he was one of them. A high roller's definition of success is knowing how to spend it after you've made it. Well, Wynn was making it and spending it with style.

How do you get Frank Sinatra to sign a three-year contract? Offer him $10 million plus stock in the company. Sinatra and gamblers, now that's an American tradition — a casino owner's New Year's Eve in July. Wynn used Sinatra's talents on and off stage. No one can fill a casino and create the excitement in a casino town like Sinatra. Wynn showed his flair for showbiz by making television commercials with Sinatra. Knowing he could never upstage Sinatra, Wynn became his straightman. The critics gave the commercials a five-star rating. How do you tell a good casino commercial from a bad one? Count the casino profits, how else! The Golden Nugget in Atlantic City won a total of $263 million in one year, setting a new world record. While most of us struggle with the smaller things in life, Wynn gave us all a chance to identify with the larger things.

With only 92 table games, Wynn went after the affluent players, like the businessman who lost $1.7 million one night playing baccarat. Sometimes called "the dapper executive," Wynn also catered to the average player. He created the "24 Karat Slot Club," the S&H Greens Stamps for the casino supermarket.

"Gambling in America is a supermarket," said Wynn. "It's a robust, whop 'em, sock 'em, screaming, table-pounding, yahoo, c'mon dice, jump up and down when you hit a jackpot. We're out to capture the fancy of Middle America, out to have fun and raise hell."

Temperamental, egocentric, impulsive, whimsical, are some words that have been used to describe Wynn. But some of his employees would disagree. Wynn treated his customers like royalty, and his employees like family. Said one employee: "He knew how to be a boss. But he also knew how to be a friend. A very good friend!"

Wynn, unlike the other casino presidents, would mingle with his dealers, valet parking attendants, waiters and waitresses, maids, all of his employees. No position was too big or too small in Wynn's eyes. Said a former dealer: "The guy could be very demanding and rude at times. But show me a casino boss who isn't and I'll show you a losing house. And I don't want to work for a loser. I've got a family to support."

"I've seen him fire people right on the spot," recalls a pit boss. "Right or wrong he knew how to run a casino. We all felt a certain loyalty working for him."

The other side of Wynn was his generosity. Thanks to Sinatra, the casino had an enormous win one week. Every employee received a bonus. "It was Christmas in July," said a hotel clerk. Once he filled a parking lot with 370 brand new cars and told his managers to each pick one. He surrounded himself with good advisers, but always had the final word. Yes he was demanding, and he had every right to be. After all, he owned the joint!

One week, Wynn gave every employee stock in the company. The employees would never see the stock split. Their market would crash, though not on Wall Street. Black Tuesday for the Golden Nugget employees came in 1986:

High rollers have a built in sense of direction when it comes to finding action! They can smell it in the air, and feel it in their souls. It's a natural instinct, a way of survival, a way of life. They turn left when everyone else turns right. In 1986, Wynn made a U-turn when Bally's decided to open up the Monopoly board one more time. Wynn sold his Atlantic City casino to Bally's for $440 million. Analysts praised his timing. Employees hugged each other and cried. It was over. The golden boy of the casino business was going to pursue his next dream.

Tonight, high above the Vegas Strip, Wynn looks out the window. Neon lights, like fireworks, flash against the dark sky. At 4 a.m. the mind becomes a junkyard of information: Mickey Mantle's lifetime batting average, the first man on the moon, Frank Sinatra's middle name, dates, addresses, and old phone numbers.

A light rain falls on the desert tonight waking up a memory. Wynn's mind drifts back to 1952 . . . a time of innocence and skinned knees. A ten-year-old boy and his father walk side by side, hand in hand, down the Vegas Strip. He remembers the Silver Slipper, and the bingo games run by his father on the second floor. Bingo by day, craps by night. That was his father's world, a world that would crumble. But the foundation would remain; his son's dream would survive.

His father died in 1963 and would never see his son's dream come true. Wynn would become one of the most successful and respected casino operators in the world. A winner beyond his wildest dreams. Steve Wynn's strength was nourished by his father's weakness. Michael Wynn's weakness was every man's dream. Father to son, dreamer to dreamer... both winners in a world built on dreams. Rest peacefully, be proud and content, your son's love is keeping the dream alive. The Mirage in the desert is no longer just an illusion!

Steve Wynn's rollercoaster ride to success may have started in Vegas. But it blossomed in Atlantic City.

The casino boom in the '80s wasn't all blue skies and sunny days. A dark cloud appeared over the Atlantic Ocean. Atlantic City would come face to face with a hurricane. The casino industry would take the brunt of the storm.

The long arm of the law was starting to reach out into the casino industry. And it looked like the Perlmans (Remember Clifford and Stuart?) were within easy reach.

Picture five people sitting in a room: a housewife, an attorney, a Ford dealership owner, and a major Merck pharmaceutical stockholder. Seated at the head of the table is a former prosecutor. The perfect setting for a

PTA meeting? A civic group? A Little League fund raiser? How about the Casino Control Commission! The five-member panel knew little about gambling, and yet their vote would determine whether or not an applicant would be granted or denied a casino license.

Four members were hired on a part-time basis and paid $18,000. Chairman Joseph Lordi was the only full-time member with a salary of $60,000. The housewife said she knew little about gambling. The heir to the Merck fortune voted *against* the gambling referendum. "Gambling was too fast," said the Ford dealer.

Atlantic City was becoming the Yankee Stadium of the casino world, and four minor-league umpires were calling balls and strikes! Someone finally came to his senses and the part-time members were replaced by four full-time members. "We still got minor league officials," said one casino manager. "Only now they're wearing glasses."

Upon leaving the commission, part-time member and pharmaceutical heir Albert Merck said: "The casino industry has the toughest and greediest people I've ever seen. They want to squeeze players for every last nickel." Keep that in mind folks the next time you pay $65 for ten pills!

The responsibility of investigating each applicant fell into the hands of the Division of Gaming Enforcement, DGE. After spending $1 million and 17 months investigating Caesars, the DGE filed a 121-page report card. Clifford Perlman didn't get a passing grade. The DGE discovered business dealings between Clifford Perlman and two alleged associates of reputed organized crime figure, Meyer Lansky.

In December of '81, the CCC decided that Caesars World and Clifford Perlman were unsuitable for licensing. William Glendon, attorney for Caesars, said that all the evidence against his client was strictly heresay. In his closing arguments, Glendon admitted that Perlman had made a mistake, but he didn't commit a crime. "What does New Jersey want?" said Glendon. "Does it want a sacrifice, an immolation?"

The Perlmans sacrificed all their stock in Caesars for $99 million and returned to Las Vegas. Caesars was granted a license.

Hugh Hefner needed four votes to be granted a casino license for his Playboy Hotel and Casino. He fell short by one vote. In 1960, Hefner was accused of bribing the New York State Liquor Authority to obtain a license for his Manhattan Playboy Club. Martin Epstein reportedly received $50,000 and L. Judson Morhouse, a Republican State Chairman reportedly received $100,000. Health reasons prevented Epstein from ever being tried. Morhouse's three-year prison sentence was commuted by New York Governor Nelson Rockefeller.

James Flanagan, the deputy director for the Division of Gaming Enforcement, pointed out that under the Casino Control Act, bribery automatically disqualifies a person or firm from obtaining a casino license. Hefner was never charged with bribery, only accused. Innocent until proven guilty? Look it up guys, it's in the Constitution.

"It is not necessary in New Jersey for a person to be indicted or convicted to find their presence is inimical in this industry," commented Walter Read prior to his appointment as chairman of the Casino Control Commission.

It cost Barron Hilton $320 million to hear those words. With three casinos in Nevada, Hilton wanted to enter the Atlantic City market. Building on an eight-acre site in the Marina, the 615-room hotel/casino would be the company's biggest undertaking to date. Hilton made one mistake: He built first and applied for a casino license second. The construction went smoothly; the CCC hearings hit nothing but stumbling blocks. The company's foundation was about to be jolted.

"Hilton Denied Gaming License." That headline sent shock waves throughout the business world. The CCC and the DGE were investigating Heinz Gunter Lewin, senior vice-president of Hilton Hotels western division, and Sidney R. Korshak, a Chicago-based attorney retained by Hilton. Investigators charged that in 1979 Lewin unlawfully comped San Francisco Teamster boss Rudy Tham at the Las Vegas Hilton. Federal judge Harry Claiborne acquitted Lewin.

Korshak's alleged ties with reputed organized crime figures put the final nail into Hilton's licensing hearing. On March 30, 1984 E. Timothy Applegate, senior vice-president and general counsel for Hilton, wrote a letter to Korshak stating: "I appreciate very much your understanding regarding the action we feel we're forced to take in dissolving the long-standing relationship between you and Hilton Hotels Corporation."

One commissioner had this to say: "The (Hilton) corporation apparently didn't get religion until it was pounding on the pearly gates of licensure."

Bally's Park Place and William O'Donnell were also "tilted." The DGE spent two years and over $2 million investigating Bally's and O'Donnell. Allegations of associating with organized crime and bribery were made against O'Donnell. Like the Perlmans, O'Donnell sold all his stock in the company and relinquished his position as chairman and company president. Robert E. Mullane replaced O'Donnell, and Bally's opened in December 1979 becoming the third casino in town.

Though faced with adversity, Atlantic City and the casino industry were growing beyond anyone's expectations... Record-breaking crowds, and unheard-of profits. Bally's, Sands, Tropicana, Del Webb, Harrah's, names synonymous with the gambling world stood high overlooking the Atlantic.

But let's not forget the pioneers: A former paint company, two guys that used to sell hot dogs, and a guy who worked his way through college running bingo games in Maryland. Could someone pass me the sauerkraut and mustard while I finish painting the kitchen? And what was that last number? B,5?

The beginning of this chapter started with the word "opportunity." Some of us play around with opportunity like a novice playing the violin by ear. But I know a guy who mastered opportunity the way Issac Stern mastered the violin. While Atlantic City was starting to settle down and find its tempo, the master was tuning up, adding a little rosin to the strings. Waiting. Watching. Listening. He would teach us all that patience isn't a virtue, it's an art!

CHAPTER 7

Talkin' 'Bout
The Boy From
New York City!

*The difference between the rich
and the rest of us — the rich
have more money.*

Ernest Hemingway

There's an unwritten social rule: never start a conversation about religion or politics. So, if your cocktail party needs a little controversy, just ask someone, "What do you think about Donald Trump?" An invisible line will divide the room in half — right wing, left wing, just like Trump's hotels. From real estate developer to casino tycoon, Trump *is* a success story with a never-ending plot.

Some financial analysts have said that the Trump Empire is on a collision course. (The Titanic of the business world?) I haven't seen Trump throwing any lifeboats overboard. Maybe a yacht here and there, but no lifeboats. Trump is a player; critics aren't. Trump buys something for $30 million and sells it for $100 million. Then some self-proclaimed financial "expert" yells, SOS. If you or I pulled off a deal like that we're geniuses! I've never heard of Trump going around an iceberg. He just plows right through them!

As a child, he used to borrow toy blocks from his brother, Robert. Gluing them together, Donald would try to build the tallest building. According to his brother, things haven't changed much. "Forty years later and he's still trying to build the tallest building."

While others are thinking about buying, Trump is closing the deal. And while one deal is closing, he's thinking about the next one. It has been said that most successful people are always one step ahead of the others. In Trump's case it's like comparing Michael Jordan's step to Dr. Ruth's. While most of us go day to day just reading the headlines, Trump looks for the rest of the story. Curiosity — that giant step into success — you're either born with it or you're not!

You're in mid-town Manhattan stuck in traffic. Listening to the news you hear: "Striking hotel employees in Vegas cause Hilton stock to slide." So what do you do? Call your broker and go long on Hilton, or short? If you're Trump, you do a little research.

Trump learned that the Hilton chain consisted of 150 hotels worldwide. But only two of those hotels were in Vegas. But, those two hotels accounted for almost 40 percent of the company's net profits. "Driver, Atlantic City, and step on it!"

Atlantic City was experiencing a casino slowdown. Many investors, after hearing about the CCC's ruling on the Perlmans, Hefner, and O'Donnell, decided to pull out of Atlantic City. The investigations were going back over 20 years. Skeletons were coming out of the closet and everyone was choking on the dust! As a result of an FBI sting operation called Abscam, Kenneth MacDonald, vice-chairman of the Casino Control Commission resigned. He admitted being present when a local politician allegedly received a $100,000 bribe from someone trying to get a casino license.

For years, Vegas lived under the cloud of organized crime. When Howard Hughes decided to buy everything in sight, the cloud disappeared. Atlantic City, in an effort to chase *their* clouds away, created a storm. Paranoia over organized crime ran rampant up and down the Boardwalk. "The worst of times often create the best opportunities to make good deals," said Trump.

If timing in life and business is everything, then Trump must have a built-in metronome. While land speculators were driving up property prices to ridiculous highs, Trump elected to sit on the sidelines and watch. But the casino business isn't a spectator sport. You don't win trophies sitting on the sidelines. Either you're a player or you're not. Trump is a player, a very high stakes player! When the home team ran up the score, Trump came off the bench.

Winter 1980! The cold wind coming in off the Atlantic Ocean echoes through abandoned construction sites. Despite the frigid weather, Atlantic City's casinos are doing record-breaking business. Trump paces the Boardwalk like an artist trying to untangle a million ideas. Lawyers, CPAs, and real estate brokers offer advice. He listens; he evaluates.

In the center of the Boardwalk, a two-and-a-half-acre piece of property becomes his canvas. His lawyers tell him that the property is a legal nightmare. But as they speak, he's already building it in his mind. Their voices become distant. They might as well be talking to the seagulls flying overhead. Floor by floor he sees what would be impossible to explain to his well-meaning advisors. Their world of liens and options are black and white. His world is in color: marble, steel, and concrete masterpieces. By July, 1981, Trump owned Atlantic City's premier piece of property. He would become Atlantic City's long-awaited child prodigy, though no one really knew it then.

Trump's credibility as a builder had reached the Jersey shore long before his limousine drove past the expressway toll plaza. His letter of introduction: New York's Trump Tower. Although Atlantic City casinos were setting new revenue highs, the construction of new hotels was in a slump. Trump, announcing that he was going to build a lavish hotel casino, became Atlantic City's designated hitter. And he didn't want to see any curve balls coming at him from the CCC (Casino Control Commission).

Previous investors, in their eagerness to open, made construction their first priority; licensing, their second. Trump would do just the opposite. Attorney Nick Ribis was hired to represent both Donald and Robert Trump at the CCC hearings. Robert, who was working for Shearson Loeb Rhodes, was Donald's first choice to oversee the Atlantic City project. Knowing that the licensing procedure could drag on for 18 months, Trump played his Trump card. He made it clear that he was willing to build in Atlantic City on a large scale. But, he was not enthusiastic about sitting around for over a year waiting for the Gaming Division to grant him a license. Trump and the officials set up a timetable: six months for a simple yes or no answer. The Gaming Division stood by their word. Six months later, the DGE (Division of Gaming Enforcement) gave the Trumps a clean bill of health.

Trump hit a solo home run his first time at bat. As he crossed home plate, Holiday Inns Inc. came running out of the Marina to shake his hand.

A few years prior, Bill Harrah, a legend in his own time, and one of the most successful casino operators in the world, came to Atlantic City. His casinos in Reno and Lake Tahoe were very profitable. Harrah died in 1978, only a few months after his decision to build in Atlantic City.

Holiday Inn, the conservative Southern Baptist hotel chain, bought a 99 percent interest in Harrah's. The deal cost Holiday Inn $300 million and its president, L.M. Clymer, who resigned because of moral beliefs. Which again brings up the question: Do gambling and religion mix? Back in the '60s, the American Farm Bureau Federation held their annual convention in Las Vegas. The one and a half million members are said to be the most conservative, Bible-pounding people in America. A Vegas spokesman had this to say: "They came with a ten-dollar bill in one hand and a copy of the Ten Commandments in the other, and didn't break either one!"

Holiday Inn was the first to build in the Marina District, away from the Boardwalk, and referred to by the locals as "the other Atlantic City." Harrah's Marina became an overnight hit with the gambling public. The company reported record-breaking earnings. Stockholders, after worrying about construction costs going millions of dollars over budget, could now sleep at night. Michael Rose, chairman of Holiday Inn, had one eye on the Boardwalk, and the other on Trump.

Rose set up a meeting with Trump. The meeting turned out to be something like "Let's Make A Deal."

Door number one: Trump would do the building. Holiday Inn would manage the casino. A 50-50 split of the profits.

Door number two: Holiday Inn would handle all the financing; they would also cough up $50 million of their own money for construction, plus $22 million in reimbursement for Trump's expenses.

Door number three: a five-year guarantee by Holiday Inn to cover any losses when the casino opened. And Trump would receive a very large construction fee!

Simply put, it was one hand washing the other. Only Trump had the larger hand. Holiday Inn needed a master builder. Trump, a rookie in the casino business, needed someone with experience.

It's easy to be a Monday-morning quarterback. But after researching Trump, one gets a certain feeling that this was not going to be a partnership made in heaven!

Born and raised in New York City, and a graduate from the Wharton School of Finance, Trump holds two degrees: one in street smarts, and the other in entrepreneurism. Throw in some ambition, imagination, and intelligence. Mix them together and you get the business world's answer to the perfect martini! Holiday Inn's management was a few months away from waking up with a hangover!

Trump's style of doing business was strictly a solo act. He was the pilot, co-pilot, and navigator. Now, for the first time in his life, he would have a flight crew — a partner. The take-off would go smoothly; the problem was landing! Trump's aggressive approach, coupled with Holiday Inn's conservative style, would create a tailspin. If I were writing for the Wall Street Journal, my headline would have read: "Corporate America's Odd Couple Play House In Atlantic City."

Holiday Inn chairman Michael Rose, like Trump, was highly respected for his leadership abilities. His reputation, like the hotel chain, had spread across the country. But being chairman of a company that trades on the New York Stock Exchange can sometimes interfere with artistic freedom. Trump could be avant-garde and abstract in his day-to-day operations. Rose had to stay within the traditional scheme. Trump was president, chairman, board of directors, and sole stockholder. Rose had to deal with the hierarchy that surrounds all publicly held companies. Two highly intelligent and astute businessmen at different ends of the spectrum. Trump and Holiday Inn made a deal. The deal from hell would make Friday the 13th look like a Disney movie.

Atlantic City's tenth casino, Harrah's Trump Plaza, opened May 14, 1984. Rose's decision to give Trump a free hand in the construction paid off. Harrah's Trump Plaza set a record before the first slot machine bell rang. It was the first casino to open on time and under budget. "A near miracle in this day and age," said Richard Goeglein, then president of Harrah's.

Although Harrah's name was first on the marquee, the spotlight followed Trump. Trump's persona gave Harrah's a built-in marketing tool. "He's his own PR guy," said Daniel Lee, analyst with Drexel Burnham Lambert. "Just look at how he builds: high-quality and glitzy." A banner over the entrance on opening day read: "New York Comes To Atlantic City." Could this be a sign of things to come?

The stockholders were happy; Rose was a hero. Holiday Inn's board of directors congratulated each other. I can only speculate that Trump had to be amused by all this. On time and under budget — for some, it's a miracle. For Trump, it's all in a day's work. And maybe for the first time he thought to himself: "Did these guys really doubt my ability?"

There was little room for doubt about the public's reaction to Atlantic City's newest casino. Every table game and slot machine was quickly filled. Maybe it was the location? Or the marketing? The Trump name might have been the drawing card for the New Yorkers. Whatever the reason, one thing became perfectly clear. This casino at the end of the expressway would become Atlantic City's centerpiece.

Trump's infatuation with Atlantic City and the casino business started to blossom. But his disenchantment with Holiday Inn management was in full bloom.

Both sides must be given credit for not turning their misunderstandings into a public mudslinging contest. Most of their problems stayed behind closed doors. Lips were sealed and doors were locked. The press knocked, but no one answered.

First, let's look at the facts. During their first month of operation, a breakdown in the accounting system occurred. A large percentage of the slot machines had to be closed. With the casino drawing record-breaking crowds, it's hard to put an exact figure on the lost revenue. It can safely be said that this error cost the casino millions of dollars. Trump was not accustomed to losing millions. Losing money wasn't part of the deal! More importantly, it wasn't the way Trump conducted business.

In December, seven months after the opening, Harrah's Trump Plaza didn't exactly light up the tote board. With ten casinos all racing to be number one, Harrah's Trump Plaza was nine lengths behind the field.

Based on these two facts, allow me to be the Sherlock Holmes of the Trump/Holiday Inn parting. Holiday Inn is one of America's largest hotel chains. When they decided to enter the gambling business, their decision to buy Harrah's was brilliant. The Harrah name alone was worth every penny. If someone said: "I was at Harrah's last night," you know they were gambling. Subconsciously, you just visualize a casino. If that same person had said: "I was at the Holiday Inn last night," you know they got a good night's sleep.

Harrah's Marina, right across from Harrah's Trump Plaza, had opened on December 20, 1980. Built and managed by Holiday Inn, they zeroed in on the slot players' market. Mr. and Mrs. Average America, the blue-collar worker, the family man. Catering to the average player is money in the bank. With the interest, they wined and dined the high rollers. The logic is simple and economically safe. History has proven that the middle-class have always been the financial backbone of our country's economic structure. Bill Harrah, the marketing genius of the casino world, had this philosophy: "I treat my customers like family. And when one of my family members win, the nieces and nephews come pay me a visit." Thanks for the memories Uncle Bill.

Corporate-run casinos are no different from corporate-run banks or insurance companies. Supervisors take orders from management. A board of directors controls management. Presidents and vice-presidents pacify stockholders. The decision-making process can take weeks or months. Endless meetings, a 60-page report that bores everyone to death, and drives secretaries crazy. By the time a decision is made the creative juice is dry. So it should surprise no one that when the corporate mentality went head to head against the old-style casino veterans, the casualty rate was high. And both sides weren't taking any prisoners. If Holiday Inn thought they had trouble with a cigar-smoking pit boss from Vegas, they would soon find out what the word "incapability" really meant.

Donald J. Trump, the pit boss of the entrepreneur game, minus the cigar smoke, would not be taken hostage. Call him arrogant, vain, mean, egotistical. But don't call him one month after the opening of Harrah's Trump Plaza Casino and tell him: "Gee Donald, because of a breakdown in the accounting system we have to close down a large percentage of our slot machines."

Knowing that the Leona Helmsleys of the hotel world have no sense of humor, Trump knew this was no practical joke. Needless to say, Trump was not amused. The idea behind owning a casino was to laugh all the way to the bank. So, what went wrong?

"Well, Donald, our supervisors are setting up a meeting with management. Management is setting up a meeting with the board members. The president is on the phone with Wall Street. And all our executive secretaries are typing a detailed report which should be on your desk in a few days. And just for the record Donald, I never believed all that stuff about you being mean, arrogant, and egotistical. Let's do lunch!"

I think Trump really lost his appetite in December when the casino reported a net loss of $241,000. Trump and Holiday Inn management weren't going door to door that year singing Christmas carols!

Put two of the world's greatest chefs in the same kitchen, and they'll argue over how to make toast! Take one very ambitious free-spirited entrepreneur, put him in a conference room with a highly successful but conservative-thinking, corporate-run management team, throw in a tablespoon of disagreement, a dash of egos, add some personality conflict, cook for one hour at 350 degrees and presto, you've got a deal burn-out!

It's no great secret that this partnership had different tastes. Trump wanted to cater to the gourmet clientele — high rollers with an never ending appetite for action. Because of their success on the Marina, Holiday Inn wanted to stick with a proven winner — the average player who occasionally went off his diet. Trump felt that he built a hotel/casino capable of attracting both sides of the gambling market with lavish suites, elegant restaurants, a sparking clean casino, plus a prime location.

High rollers, aside from the obvious fact that they tend to gamble and lose large sums of money, are part of a casino's magnet. People love to mingle among the rich.

Where else can you see someone lose $100,000, and then order a brandy without blinking an eye? It's America's biggest spectator-sport playing to eager crowds in casinos throughout the world! While Holiday Inn was conducting marketing surveys, Trump was ordering brandy snifters — by the carload!

Because of Trump's financial status, he traveled and rubbed elbows with the elite. Rich and influential, he had all the makings to become the world's most valuable casino host. Holiday Inn had a built-in American Express customer-list of potential high rollers. Trump's ability to attract the million-dollar player was an asset to the casino and leverage for Trump. And if there's one thing that Trump understands, it's leverage. He never leaves home without it!

It's 11:59 p.m. Thousands of people with funny hats and unrealistic expectations crowd Times Square. On this night, no one is a stranger. Loneliness, disguised as hope and promise, mingle in with the crowd. Dreams are at bargain-basement prices tonight. A clearing-house sale, a once-a-year sellathon where everything must go and nothing is refundable. Promises, although sincere, have loopholes. Thirty seconds away from acceptable lunacy and counting. Each second edges us on, teasing us with ambition and false hope. Resolutions, like commandments, were made to be obeyed, but forgiven if broken. Across America the countdown begins. Television announcers wearing tuxedos sound like carnival hawkers selling tickets to the midway attraction.

Millions of people brace themselves for that magic moment. Ten, nine, eight, yes I will quit smoking. Seven,

six, five, I promise to lose weight. Four, three, two —
quick, pass me a match and a doughnut! Happy New
Year!

Should old acquaintance be forgot and never brought
to mind? I don't know if Trump has much of a singing
voice, but one thing is certain, he knows how to inter-
pret a lyric! His first decision for the New Year: buy out
my partners!

As for Holiday Inn management, they, too, were singing, a corporate sing-a-long — just follow the bouncing
deal! This was one New Year's resolution that both sides
could agree on. The partnership from hell was knocking
on the door to purgatory. A mortal business sin would
finally be forgiven. The penance: a two-year waiting
period.

In May of 1986, Trump became the sole owner of
Trump Plaza Hotel and Casino. Trump went after the
best management team money could buy. Stephen Hyde,
executive vice president and chief operating officer at the
Golden Nugget, became Trump's new general manager.
On Hyde's recommendation, Trump assembled an all-
star Atlantic City management team. Trump's offer of
higher pay and bonus incentives, created a mutiny among
casino personnel. Casinos up and down the Boardwalk
were yelling: "Man overboard." With Trump at the
helm, the Plaza turned a profit of $58 million for the
year!

Meanwhile, back at their Memphis headquarters, all
was calm and profitable. Holiday Inn, no longer partners with Trump, concentrated on their Marina property.
Establishing a loyal following of "better people," Harrah's Marina was becoming a constant winner. Their mar-

keting program, plus a solid employee morale, gave Harrah's the edge in this very competitive business. They created an atmosphere where customers could relate to each other, and employees, especially dealers, could relate to the customers. With college degrees hanging in every office, it still reverted back to Bill Harrah's wisdom: "Treat everyone like family." Higher education sometimes comes from the least educated.

But the safe waters flowing into the Marina would soon become shark-infested. A shark was circling, and by the time someone yelled HELP, it was almost too late. Nothing like a little hostile takeover to ruin someone's summer vacation!

Looking to tread deeper waters, Trump started to accumulate stock in Holiday Inn. Starting in August, Trump began purchasing large blocks of Holiday Inn shares. By September, Trump accumulated over one million shares, or nearly five percent of the company. Some have speculated that Trump's attempt to gain control of Holiday Inn was an act of revenge. Selling at $54 a share in late August, most Wall Street analysts believed that Holiday Inn was a prime candidate for a takeover attempt. When the stock hit $76 a share in November, Trump sold. Revenge, or good business? Or maybe just a high roller looking for a little *action*!

For every action there's a reaction! Holiday Inn wasn't about to sail off into the sunset without a fight. Instead of running, they dropped anchor and battened down the hatches. Michael Rose and Holiday management, behind closed doors in Memphis, worked out a plan to stop Trump's takeover move. It would cost Holiday Inn over $2.6 billion to calm the seas. Through bank financing and selling some of its assets, the company reduced its larger than life debt. The revamping of the company lead the way for the newly formed Promus Companies. Holiday stockholders received stock in the new company. Promus Companies would now consist of five Harrah's casinos, Embassy Suites, Hampton Inns, and Homewood Suites. Everyone walked away with a piece of the pie. Donald Trump and Holiday Inn management finally did lunch! Only Trump started with the dessert first.

When Hilton was denied a casino license, the news hit Hilton's corporate headquarters like an earthquake, sending the boardmembers running for shelter. Hilton already had two strikes against it. In 1959, their Carte Blanche credit card business cost the company millions. In 1967, they sold their international hotel division for stock in TWA, which was selling for about $90 a share. OPEC threw strike two; seven years later TWA stock was worth $5 a share.

Trump decided to call Barron Hilton in California. One businessman calling another in his time of need. The price for this long distance call — $320 million.

With all the problems facing Trump and his Holiday Inn partnership, nothing could distract him from sensing a deal! Before hanging up, Trump made it clear that if Hilton was interested in selling, Trump might be interested in buying. Benjamin Lambert, a friend of Trump's, was hosting a party for the Hilton board and invited Trump to attend. With the company's annual meeting only a few days away, this was one invitation Trump couldn't turn down. On a cold winter night in March, Barron Hilton and Donald Trump met face to face for the first time. The party took place in Manhattan, but the party crasher was in Atlantic City.

Trumpmania, Round Two

"Ladies and gentlemen, may I present the challenger. Fighting out of Las Vegas, wearing a $2,000 suit, and smoking a Dunhill Montecristo No. 1 cigar. Ladies and gentlemen, the golden boy of the casino world, Steve Charis... ma Wynn."

In was inevitable that Wynn and Trump would someday go head to head. Judging this main event, which started in April, would not be easy. Stockbrokers, Hilton board members, stockholders, all had something to gain or lose on the outcome. Wynn, looking for a first round knockout, offered to buy 27.4 percent of Hilton stock which was owned by the estate of Conrad Hilton. With the stock selling in the high sixties, Wynn's offer of $72 a share, brought the shareholders to their feet. Barron, who was refereeing the bout, yelled low blow. Hilton's board members agreed. Trump was only interested in buying the Hilton property in Atlantic City. Wynn was trying to buy the company. And in doing so, Wynn brought Barron right into Trump's corner. Without realizing it, Wynn was doing Trump a favor. A favor that Trump would someday return.

The media played up the event, calling it ego vs. ego. In reality it was nothing more than two Wharton School graduates having a spat. Unnoticed by almost everyone was the fact that Trump and Wynn weren't against the ropes, Barron was. And no one from Hilton wanted to be the first to throw in the towel.

The fight ended when Trump threw in a check for $320 million. Buying the property sight-unseen, Trump Castle would become trophy number two.

When you're hot, you're hot, and Trump was boiling over with takeover fever. In November and December 1986, Trump bought 3,057,000 shares of Bally stock. Fearing that Trump would take over the company, Bally's sued. Trump countersued, checkmate. Bally's, knowing that no one could legally own more than three casinos, bought the Golden Nugget from Steve Wynn. If Trump took over Bally's, he would be one casino over the limit. The deal cost Bally's nearly $500 million. Steve Wynn went to Vegas to build his Mirage. Trump made a profit of over $20 million when he sold his 9.9 percent stake back to Bally's.

The dealings gave Trump a front-row seat in the corporate management production. When the curtain came down, there were no standing ovations. Reviews were mixed. But now, with two casinos playing to packed houses every night, Trump was center stage. With the magnetism of Sir Lawrence Olivier playing Hamlet, Trump delivered this line for all to hear: "To buy, or not to buy, that is not the question, that is the *art*."

Only in the casino business a few years, Trump had the old pros sitting up and taking notes. The laws governing casino ownership in New Jersey state that no single company or single individual can own more than three casinos. Trump didn't want to break the law, he just wanted to follow it to the fullest. He was one deal away from his third casino. And one billion dollars away from the Eighth Wonder of the World!

Trumpmania, Round Three

Resorts International founder, James Crosby, died in 1986, leaving behind his dream of building the world's largest casino, the Taj Mahal. His family decided to sell their $101 million interest in the company. With construction on the Taj already millions over budget, the family realized that a $600 million dream was too much for them to handle. The family rejected the $135-a-share offer made by Pratt Hotel Corp. Respecting Crosby's dream, the family wanted someone with an expertise in building to turn the dream into a reality. Trump, matching Pratt's offer, became the family's choice. "I have a tremendous expertise in building," said Trump. "That's why I was the one."

Even though the family received higher offers from outside bidders, they stuck to their agreement with Trump. Trump's wheel of fortune was spinning. Round and round she goes and where she stops only Vanna White knows! And speaking of game shows...

> *The Final Jeopardy Answer Is:*
> *He parlayed a $50 record date into $300 million. Remember to phrase your answer in the form of a question.*
> *Who is Merv Griffin?*
> *Correct!*

Did Trump put Griffin in "final jeopardy" by selling him Resorts International? (Trump would keep the unfinished Taj Mahal, however, as his "jewel" in the deal.) The Wall Street Journal and other financial publications have been debating this issue since day one.

Casino analyst Marvin Roffman said: "Merv got raked over the coals." One business magazine wrote a story titled: How Donald Trump Taught Merv the Art of the Deal. *People* magazine, which knows business like Barrons knows Madonna's latest record, said: Merv got the better deal.

Selling Resorts cleared the way for Trump to finish construction on the Taj. It was no secret that Griffin had his eye on the casino business years before the Trump deal. But buying Resorts for $325 million would now pose another question: Were Merv Griffin's eyes bigger than his bankbook?

No one can say that Griffin is a bad businessman. At 64, this self-made millionaire was ready to face a new challenge. The casino business seemed perfectly suited for Merv. Casinos are entertainment; Merv is an entertainer. Worth more than $300 million, his creative energy in radio and television are major achievements. In his deal with Coke, Griffin negotiated a contract giving him 35 percent of all syndication revenue from "Wheel of Fortune" and "Jeopardy." His deal with Trump wouldn't be that lucrative. Buying a casino buried in debt isn't exactly fun and games.

Open Sesame
April 5, 1990

Politicians smiling and shaking hands squeeze through the crowd. Celebrities sign autographs and pose for pictures. Even the high rollers in the front-row seats are impressed by the extravaganza. "It looks like a high-roller convention," said a man wearing a cowboy hat. "There's enough money in the first ten rows to balance the country's budget!''

A young woman asks, "Which one is Donald Trump?" A man smoking a cigar with a heavy New York accent answers, "He's the guy with all the money."

A tape recording of "I've Got a Lovely Bunch of Coconuts" is all the introduction the next speaker needs. Climbing the steps to the podium, the elbow-to-elbow crowd applauds. The years of endless one-night stands and forgotten ballrooms have been kind to him. Looking younger than his age, he quickly walks to the microphone. The stress and strain of legal and financial hassles has not dulled his sense of humor. As the music fades, Merv Griffin delivers the one-liner that brings the house down: "I *used* to have a lot of coconuts."

Standing before an enormous Aladdin's lamp, Donald Trump, the Houdini of the casino world, demonstrated his magical powers. Fabu, the ethereal genie appeared on a large screen as Trump rubbed the lamp. "Stars and Stripes Forever" came blaring over the sound system. Above the patriotic theme, fireworks and laser lights flashed across the darkened sky. "It's like the Fourth of July and New Year's Eve rolled into one," said one spectator. Reporters from around the world and across the country ran to pay-phones. Tomorrow, everyone (except those living on Mars) will have read about Trump's Taj Mahal.

An elderly man summed up the night by saying: "I've lived here for 86 years. Born and raised three blocks from here. I was eight years old when the Miss America Pageant started. The Steel Pier, Steeplechase Pier, the Million Dollar Pier, I've seen them come and go. But this place, the Taj Mahal, has to be the biggest event to hit Atlantic City since the end of World War II.''

Fourteen years of planning, and over six years in construction, Trump's billion dollar casino was Atlantic City's booster shot! Architect Francis X. Dumont's eight-year devotion to the Taj project was now complete. Over 100,000 people came to the Taj that night. If the fireworks outside seemed loud, the fireworks inside would make them sound like firecrackers.

When the casino opened on a Monday for an eight-hour test run, the slot machines won $713,000. That's $89,125 an hour, or $1,485 a minute, give or take a quarter here and there. Even the change machines ran out of money.

The high-volume play caused so many problems that many of the machines had to be closed. Many tabloid writers took a sucker-punch at Trump. ''The Eighth Blunder of the World,'' became headlines. In their zealous quest to deck Trump, the headline hunters missed the real story. The Taj Mahal smashed every casino record in the world! Three days after opening, the table-games alone had an estimated drop of $7.5 million.

To break even, the casino had to generate over $1 million a day. The slot machine breakdown sent most executives running for cover. At $89,000-an-hour, we're not talking minimum wage. Vice president of finance Donald C. Wood collapsed from exhaustion. Hotel president Walter Haybert was demoted and replaced Wood. Donald Buzney, vice president of personnel, was fired.

At 37 years of age, Edward Tracy became the new president and chief executive officer of Trump's three casinos. Willard ''Bucky'' Howard became the new president and CEO of the Taj Mahal. "As a casino operator, Bucky is one of the best," said Trump in a statement to the press. Trump finally assembled his "A" team. All he needed now was a winning season. But the visiting team didn't arrive by bus. They came in a Trojan horse.

When we think of June, we think of Father's Day, graduations, and the start of summer. But in June of 1990, one more item had to be added to the list: "Trump-Bashing." Sensing that his financial empire might be suffering a wound, the media came in for the kill. For over a month, every major publication and gossip-type news show ran a story on Trump. Keeping the public informed is one thing, but shoving it down their throats creates a three-ring circus where the lions are kept unfed and uncaged.

Trump, by his own ingenuity, made himself a superstar. In doing so, he also made a lot of people envious of his wealth and power. America loves a winner, but loathes a bragger! But isn't bragging a form of advertising? Walt Disney Productions spent millions of dollars on advertisements to hype-up the public for their summer release, Dick Tracy. Financial analysts call this creative advertising. But when Trump tells the world, "My casinos are the best," he's called a rich, loud-mouth, egotistical brat!

Comic Relief

The public, growing bored with the facts and figures, needed a laugh. Garry Trudeau, in his "Doonesbury" comic strip, had Trump standing on the ledge of Trump Tower. A crowd of onlookers standing below were urging him to jump. And who said Andrew Dice Clay was vulgar?

New York Daily News columnist, Gail Collins, wrote: "We are about to have one of those magic New York moments where people of all creeds, races, and economic backgrounds join together in a single thought: Hehehe-hehehe."

"At last, all of us who've so loved the game of kicking Trump while he's up will have the fiendish thrill of kicking Trump while he's down." Robert Reno, columnist for New York Newsday.

Trump, who liked to put his name on everything he owned — Trump Shuttle, Trump Tower, Trump Card (the game show), Trump Princess (the yacht), Trump Plaza, Trump this, Trump that — suddenly found his name in the headlines with every writer striving for the most clever alliteration and rhyme. The Donald in Disarray, Slump de Trump, The Trump Thump, Trump Takes His Lumps, How Trump Got Bumped, Trump Stumped, and Trump Dumped (the divorce).

Even comedian David Letterman jumped on the Trump-Wagon (sorry) with his "top 10" list of signs that Trump is in trouble. The No. 1 sign, said Letterman: "He now takes my calls."

It's ironic how so many publications followed Trump's selling tactic. By using hype-type headlines, their sales rose. The very same sword that Trump used against his competitors was now in the hands of the dragon. The King took refuge in his Castle and threw a party. The uninvited dragon would huff and puff, but could not blow the door down.

Happy Birthday

On June 14, 1990, Donald Trump celebrated his 44th birthday. His horoscope, according to Stella Wilder, read as follows: "Born today, you are a confident and even cocky individual who will make a career out of doing what others say can't be done, and reaching goals others say are out of reach.

"You have a sixth sense that impresses people, and when you set out to impress people you go right for the throat! There will never be any doubt about your abilities in any field, once you begin displaying them freely."

Are there any astrologers working for Chase Manhattan, Bankers Trust, Citicorp, or Manufacturers Hanover?

At 8 a.m., on Saturday morning, June 16, 1990, hundreds of people are gathered together on the boardwalk in front of the Taj. There are no picket signs, no anti-slogans. It's a demonstration of love and loyalty. A support group and belated birthday wish, rolled into one. Employees of the Trump Organization, many just getting off work, have come to rally around their boss, Donald Trump.

"It's a grassroots show of support by all the employees at the Trump properties in Atlantic City," said Marc Goldberg, vice president of advertising for the Taj.

Standing before the crowd, his eyes showing the emotion of the moment, Trump gave these comments: "We're setting every record at the Taj. Nobody wants to write about the positive. They just want to write about the negatives. We'll just keep setting records, and maybe they'll write about that."

After a spontaneous sing-along version of "Happy Birthday" from the crowd, Trump gave his closing comment: "Over the years I've surprised a lot of people. And the biggest surprise is yet to come."

Over 1,000 high rollers and personal friends attended Trump's 44th birthday party that night at Trump Castle. I didn't attend the party. My invitation probably got lost in the mail. When the party ended, I was standing outside the Crystal Ballroom. As the guests filed out, photographers took aim. People who spend thousands on designer clothes in order to appear as if they weren't designed at all, emerged from the ballroom. As Trump's security guards cleared a path, the birthday-boy appeared. Trump, showing no signs of stress or strain, smiled to the crowd. Shaking hands with a few well-wishers, he disappeared into the casino.

Three days later I'm watching television. A bulletin appears on the bottom of the screen. It read: "Donald Trump no longer owns the world's largest hotel. Details at 11."*

On June 19, 1990, Circus Circus Enterprises Inc. opened the 4,032-room Excalibur Hotel on the Vegas Strip.

"Ladies and gentlemen and children of all ages, step right up for the greatest show on earth. Watch in amazement as Donald Trump performs his high-wire act without a net. He'll excite and incite you. His debt-defying feats know no bounds. Watch as bondholders, banks, the Pratt Hotel Corp. and a host of others shake the very

---

*Technically, the Taj Mahal never was the "world's largest hotel." It does, however, have the largest casino.

wire Trump is trying to walk. Will he tumble and fall? Or will he show the world, once and for all, that you don't make it to the Big Top working with a safety net!''

Trump's book, titled: ''Trump: Surviving at the Top,'' might just be the final epitaph for all those skeptics who, like the gutless craps player, never took the odds!

CHAPTER 8

Comedy Club

People who go through life with a net under them suddenly become daredevils when they enter a casino. Evel Knievels with a hundred bucks in their pocket perform thousand-dollar stunts. A man, who wouldn't consider anything but a safe mutual fund investment, just pressed his fifth losing blackjack bet. His wife, who two days ago drove five miles out of her way just to save five cents on a gallon of gas, plays a $5 slot machine.

From the mezzanine, the casino floor offers us an entertaining view of human behavior. Most of us may recall a film in high-school science class where a mouse, finding his way through a maze, is rewarded with a small piece of cheese. For a moment, picture the casino floor as a maze, with endless aisles of slot machines and table games. Players, searching for that piece of cheese, run through the maze, bumping into slot machines and side-swiping tables in a desperate attempt to find their reward.

A slot player puts five coins in a machine and gets back zilch, then moves to another machine. Craps players lose three pass-line bets in a row and scurry to another table. Casino people call this "table-hopping." After losing two double-downs, a player wins a small hand, loses another, and heads for the nearest lounge. In a few minutes, he'll be back at the tables.

Remember the fairy tale about Hansel and Gretel? When entering the forest they left behind a trail of bread crumbs to help guide them safely home. But their plan was foiled when hungry birds ate the trail. In the petrified forest of a casino, players also leave a trail... of chips, coins, and markers. From table to table, from slot machine to slot machine, the most traveled paths, unfortunately, are the ones leading to the doors and to the elevators.

And just like the laboratory mouse who never seems satisfied with his reward, we continue to run through the maze until we're either exhausted or broke! M-I-C-, see you real soon, K-E-Y, why, because we like you. L-O-S-E-R.

If we can get through all of this and still have the ability to laugh at ourselves, then we've found the golden path. There is no other public gathering place that offers unrehearsed, spur-of-the-moment comedy every night of the week. Nameless comics headline the casino floor without billing. Slap-stick and stand-up, with an endless array of one-liners. Let me introduce you to the casino's Comedy Club:

Stand By Your Man

A man wearing a black suit and black silk shirt walks over to a 21 table. Around his neck are four gold chains, one with a crucifix. Around his pinky is a gold ring with a crucifix. Around his arm is a very sexy and beautiful blonde. (If this guy is a priest, I'm ready to take the vows.) His date's dress is no bigger than a matchbook cover. Heads from three tables away turn to look at her.

The man reaches into his pocket and pulls out (you guessed it) a gold money clip, minus the crucifix. He counts out 23 one-hundred-dollar bills, which doesn't put a dent in his bankroll. "Gimme two thousand in black and three hundred in green."

Turning to the blonde, he said, "Sit down and play!" Trying very hard to squeeze into a seat without revealing that which hasn't already been revealed, the blonde answered, "But I never played this game before."

"Don't worry about a thing. I'll tell you what to do," said her knight in gold armor. "Just remember one thing. If you get 17, stand."

Betting $100 a hand for himself and $25 for his girl-friend, the game began. About six hands later, the blonde is dealt a King and a 7. Fighting for every inch, she manages to stand up. Her date looked at her with a confused expression. "What the hell's a matter? Whatja stand up for?" The blonde, pausing for a second, said, "Honey, you told me to stand if I got 17!"

32 Across

"I'll tell you a couple of stories," said Phil, a craps dealer for 18 years. "One night my table is really cooking. The shooter's on a hot roll. The betting is at a fast pace. A player rushing to get a bet in gets tongue-tied. All of a sudden his false teeth fall out and bounce onto the table. The boxman, who was a little nuts, pulls out *his* false teeth and throws them on the table saying, 'Sir, you got a bet!' "

"I'm working the stick one night. A lady built like Dolly Parton in a low-cut dress is having a ball. She's a nickel bettor with enthusiasm, jumping up and down on every roll of the dice. The shooter was at the opposite end of the table. As the dice hit the table, one of them bounced off and went right between, uh, the valley of the dolls! Every man at the table offered to assist her in finding the missing die. She was a good sport, joking right back at them, but she came up empty in her search for it.

New dice were put in the game. The incident did little to dull her enthusiastic spirit. Like a cheerleader, she continued to jump up and down rooting for numbers. About five minutes later the dice hit the wall and presto, there's three dice on the table. The missing die must have gotten loose and popped out of her bra. In a loud clear voice I said, '15, and it came the hard way!' "

Honesty Is The Best Policy

A man acting very macho thought he was being cute one night. Standing next to the stickman, who happened to be a woman, Mr. Macho Man was clearly making a pass at her. It was obvious that she wasn't interested. Remaining cool and professional, she did her best to ignore his stupid remarks.

"I got a prop bet for you, honey," said Mr. Macho Man as he threw a green chip toward the object of his affection. In a very seductive voice he said, "A hard ten, how's that sound, sweetheart?" The girl said nothing as she placed the bet. Three rolls later the shooter throws a hard four. The stickgirl, making sure everyone at the table could hear, looked Macho Man right in the eye and said, "You know, sometimes it pays to be honest!"

The Dallas Cowboy Crapshooter

A pit boss tells this story: "We had a high roller who thought that the harder he threw the dice, the more passes he would make. One of the dealers gave him the nickname 'Cockeye,' because the dice would sometimes fly all over the casino. Players standing at the other end of the table would duck for cover when Cockeye was the shooter.

One night, a player got hit in the eye by one of Cockeye's unguided missiles. But the injured player, who was threatening to sue, made a miraculous recovery when Cockeye gave him a $500 chip. Malpractice, casino-style.

Cockeye and I were both born in Texas, and in his eyes we were brothers. He insisted on playing in my pit. One Superbowl weekend Cockeye flew in on his private jet. He gave me eleven Dallas Cowboy sweatshirts as a gift which gave me an idea. On the day of the game I went out and bought six Dallas Cowboy helmets. As the game entered the fourth quarter I was informed that Cockeye would be playing in my pit. We posted the $1,000 minimum sign and waited.

Ten minutes after the game ended, Cockeye and three other players opened the table. Two shooters later, the dice went to Cockeye. As Cockeye got ready to throw the dice, the dealers and I put on the football helmets. The three other players had no idea what was going on. Cockeye just held the dice for a second, looking at me and the dealers.

Suddenly, he became a sportscaster: 'Staubach scrambles looking for a receiver. Dorset is deep. The throw.' Cockeye would then throw the dice as if they were a football. The dice would bounce off the helmets and onto the table. Oh yeah, Dallas won the Superbowl. And Cockeye lost $147,000.''

Right Place, Wrong Time

Being in the right place at the right time! Does that statement separate the winners from the losers? On a cold December night it did.

Walking through the casino one night I saw a craps table roped off. Reserved signs were posted on the $500 minimum table. The floorman told me that the table was reserved for ten players flying in from New York. At nine o'clock the action began. Two hours later the casino won $175,000. I think I heard the stickman say, ''Pay the line,'' twice.

The table, now empty, went back to a $5 minimum. Five minutes later, a player with a $50 buy-in holds the dice for almost 30 minutes. He left the table with $575. The pit boss, who had noticed me standing there for almost three hours said: ''You just witnessed the ultimate definition of the old cliche, ''Being in the right place at the right time.''

To Tell The Truth

A change-person told me this story. ''The progressive jackpot on our carousel of dollar machines was over $137,000. I kept making change for a player who sat at the same machine for over five hours. I guess he put close to $800 into that machine. He asked the slot host for a dinner comp and left.

I guess he was looking at the menu when it happened. Because ten minutes later a woman, playing the same machine, hit the jackpot.

After dinner, the man came back to play at the same machine. As I was changing his hundred-dollar bill, he noticed that the $137,000 had been hit. 'When did that happen?' he asked.

What do you tell a guy who just missed hitting a $137,650 jackpot by ten minutes? A lie, that's what you tell him.

'About 30 minutes after you left, someone a few machines away hit it.'

'A few machines? Where?'

'Well, no, actually, he was in the next aisle over.'

'Next aisle?'

'You know, I think he was clear over on the other side of the casino.'

'Oh. Someone hit my machine, huh?'

Monkey See, Monkey Do

Most people assume that big bettors really know how to play. Nothing could be further from the truth. I've seen blackjack players betting $1,000 a hand doubling down on a hard twelve, and craps players making $1,000 field bets.

I decided to do a little experiment to prove how easy it is to sway people's judgment. A roulette table would serve as my testing ground. Two friends of mine, who are actors, were my lab technicians. One would play the part of a mathematician, dressed in a conservative suit, glasses, and smoking a pipe. Two notebooks with meaningless calculations and equations were his props. Wearing a tuxedo, friend number two played the James Bond-type high roller.

I figured that if we could win three bets in a row, the other players would follow our betting pattern. Easier said than done. Two casinos later, and down $200, we finally connected.

Watching the wheel, the mathematician began writing down the outcome. About ten spins later, he told "007" to bet red. The $100 bet on red opened a few eyes at the $5 minimum table. We won the bet. A few spins later we bet $100 on black and won. We now had the audience in the palm of our hand.

They watched and listened as the mathematician, with eyes glued to his notebook, said, "The conversion factor is positive, bet odd." When the ball fell into 23, even *I* started believing the mathematician.

"Don't bet until the ratio factor is level," said the mathematician. (Was this method-acting or what?) Three spins later he said, "Bet black; the ratio leveled out." The entire table bet black. The entire table also lost.

But their confidence wasn't deflated. They copied our next four bets, winning only one.

Leaving the table one man asked: "Where did you learn to gamble like that?" My friend answered: "The Lee Strasberg Theater Institute."

No Roll, Die Overboard, Abandon Ship!

"No roll, die down," those four words create havoc at a craps table. It's like yelling "fire" in a crowded movie theater. But in a casino, no one runs for the exit. Instead, they hose down the burning inferno with superstition. "Same dice. Take my bets down. Off on the next roll." What's that, you can't find the missing die? Call in the FBI, and the CIA. Bring in the bloodhounds.

Men who never think of bending down to pick up a sock when walking through their homes, are on all fours crawling around looking for that missing die. High above the casino floor, the eye in the sky watches. "They look like a bunch of ants searching for a sugar cube," said one security guard.

Is that missing die playing hide-and-seek just to save the casino money? Let's listen in on the conversation going on at the table.

Player 1: "The shooter's working for the house. He threw the die off the table to jinx the players."

Player 2: "You think so?"

Player 3: "Hey, they have guys working the blackjack tables. They walk around all day hitting 16's against a dealer's five."

Player 2: "Yeah, they split tens, too."

Player 4: "I don't believe it!"

Player 5: "Believe it, pal. They're disguised as tourists."

Player 6: "I knew there was something about the shooter that rubbed me the wrong way."

Player 7: "Why me, why me? I finally press up my bets and then this happens."

Player 8: "Maybe it was an accident."

Player 9: "Accident my foot. The guy made six passes and then throws a die off the table. He's a casino plant."

Player 10: "I heard this joint might file for Chapter 11."

Player 11: "It's a conspiracy. Where's the CCC and the DGE?"

Player 12: "I need a drink."

Twelve angry men face to face with the casino justice system. Five minutes ago they all seemed like intelligent and rational people. That missing die turned them into a lynch mob.

Eyes, bloodshot with fear, twitch in pain as the shooter reaches for the new dice. Players, anticipating the worst, squeeze the railing until their knuckles turn white. Hail Marys and Our Fathers are silently recited at record-breaking speed. The shooter wants to pick up the odds behind his pass-line bet. Knowing this could cause a riot, he decides to brave it out. Two players sigh in relief as the shooter wipes his sweaty hand on the green felt. "Don't worry," said one player to his friend, "this guy knows what he's doing."

Trying to restore order, the stickman informs the table: "Nine's the point. The shooter has the dice. Hands high." The shooter, with dice in hand, recalls a line from the movie Wall Street: "Well... life all comes down to a few moments, and this is one of 'em..." As the dice leave his hand, someone yells: "I found it. I found it. I found the missing die!"

In the casino world of justice it's too little too late. Circumstantial evidence doesn't sway the jury's decision. The people and the state rest their case. The dice have hit the "walls" of justice!

Ladies and gentlemen of the jury, have you reached a verdict? There will be no hung jury tonight. No surprise witness. No Perry Mason ending. The stickman stands before the crowded court and reads the verdict: "Craps, two aces."

Justice has been served. Innocent by reason of insanity! The shooter is hereby sentenced to throw the dice again.

"If dice have no brains," said one dealer, "where does that leave the player?"

The answer to that question might be on the Boardwalk. Angelo and Flip work the afternoon crowd on the boards. Children, as well as adults, are fascinated by their routines. As a team, they perform magic tricks with astounding speed. Working solely on tips, Flip accepts quarters from the crowd. The crowd-pleaser and star of the show, Flip demonstrates his dexterity when throwing dice.

Overhand, underhand, right-handed, left-handed, overhead, around his back, dice fly onto a miniature craps table. Angelo calls all the rolls which generate applause from the crowd every time Flip makes his point. Sometimes Flip gets overly enthusiastic and his aim is a little off. Any die falling into the crowd gets to be someone's souvenir, like a foul ball at a baseball game.

One afternoon, I watched Flip make nine passes in a row. I would love to be at a table when Flip gets the dice. But that's impossible unless the casinos change their rules.

You see, Flip is a monkey.

Matchmaker, Matchmaker

Some casinos have steady customers... regulars. Some players come once a week on the same day. These calendar-type players get to know each other and friendships develop. Every Tuesday, a man in his early 30s and a married couple in their 60s played blackjack at the same table. They began to socialize, going out for dinner together with the winner picking up the tab. If all three lost, it was dutch-treat. When the married couple learned that the young man was single, the wife began telling him about their daughter. A blind date was arranged.

Meeting in the casino for the first time, it was love at first sight. Six months later they were married. After returning from their honeymoon, the new groom came to Atlantic City that following Tuesday alone. Seeing his mother-in-law at a table the newlywed walked over and kissed her hello. "Mom, I've got great news." But the mother-in-law wasn't smiling. "What the hell are you doing here?" she asked. Confused by her sudden change in personality, the son-in-law said nothing. "If you think you're gonna come here every Tuesday, and blow two hundred bucks, you've got another thing coming. I didn't raise my daughter so that she could marry a bum!"

"But Mom, I hit a slot jackpot for $65,000."

"Harry, Harry," screamed the mother-in-law to her husband who was two tables away. "Harry, look, our darling son-in-law is here."

The Flying Carpet

"I've only been dealing craps in Atlantic City for two weeks," said Bill. "But I worked in Reno for seven years. So let me tell you a Reno story.

We got a hot shooter at my table one night. At the opposite end of the table we got a human jumping-jack. This guy was jumping up and down, yelling and screaming. Sweat was pouring down his forehead. Something about the guy didn't look right to me but I couldn't put my finger on it. All of a sudden this thing comes flying off his head. His toupee falls on the table and covers one of the dice. It happened so fast that the stickman couldn't make the call. So now we got one die showing and the other is under this guy's rug. The point was ten, and the one up die was showing a five.

The stickman froze; the boxman was silent. No one knew what to do. I mean what's the ruling if a guy's toupee falls on a die? Suddenly, one player started yelling: 'The roll counts, lift up the wig.' The entire table joined in chanting: 'Roll counts, roll counts.' With the uncovered die showing five, I guess they figured half the point was there.

The bald headed guy's wife was laughing as she said: 'Great Joe, you blow $5,000 gambling and won't spend more than $200 on a rug.'

'We'll talk about this later, Ruth. The hell with the toupee. I've got a $50 hard ten working.'

The pit boss decided to let the roll count. Like a surgeon performing open-heart surgery, the stickman very slowly removed the toupee from the die. The operation was successful. 'Ten, and it came the hard way,' said Ben Casey with a toupee hanging off the stick.

The stickman passed the toupee to the player and the dice to the shooter. 'Ruth, $350 and that ain't countin' my pass-line bet,' said the unembarrassed player. Taking his toupee off the stick, the man tucked it safely away in his back pocket.

'Great,' said the man's wife. 'I always suspected your brains were back there. Now, after 27 years of marriage you proved my point!' ''

All In The Family

The daughter of a very high-rolling craps player had a very unusual wedding day. The wedding ceremony, followed by a lavish reception, was to take place two floors above the casino in the ballroom. The bride's father, who had a credit line for $500,000, wanted nothing but the best for his only daughter. He booked 50 rooms for friends and relatives. The hotel's gourmet chef would prepare a special meal. Three bands would provide dance music. Flowers arrived by the truckload. This would truly be a day to remember for all in attendance.

Dressed and pacing up and down, the nervous groom had a little over an hour before taking the vows of holy matrimony. One of the ushers suggested that the groom and a few of the guys go down to the casino and play for a while. With tuxedos on, and bow ties in place, the groom and two ushers decide to play craps.

An hour later, the groom was on a hot roll with dice in hand. Upstairs in the ballroom, the invited guests sat waiting for the ceremony to begin. One hundred people were looking at their watches, as if a bomb were set to go off. The bride and her mother were in tears. The groom's parents were embarrassed. The preacher had another drink. The temperamental chef complained that his dinner would be ruined by the delay. The band played another bossa nova. The bride's father contemplated murder while two floors below, the groom was murdering the don't-pass bettors.

Sensing mayhem, the best man told the bride's father where his new, and/or "late," son-in-law might be found. Storming into the casino with blood in his eyes, he headed right for the crowded craps table. "My daughter is upstairs crying her eyes out and you're down here shooting craps. I'll kill you, you little..."

"But sir," said one of the ushers. "He's made ten passes in a row!"

"Ten," said the bride's father, his voice still in a rage.

"Come on. Let's get the game moving," said one of the players.

"Take it easy, Mr. B.," said a floor person trying to restore calm at the table.

"I'm sorry, I'm sorry," said the groom. "Someone else shoot. I'm late for my own wedding."

"Just a minute, son," said the bride's father as he pulled out $5,000 in cash. "Keep shootin'. "

Ten minutes later, the bride's mother and the groom's parents found them at the table. A pre-family feud was about to take place. By the time law and order was restored, the bride's father won $54,000.

Turning to his wife, the bride's father proudly proclaimed: "Martha, we're not only gaining a son today, we're getting a *shooter* in the family!"

McSheik

"I had a player from Arabia," said a roulette dealer. "He was the nephew of some sheik. His uncle gave him $2 million for the weekend. A little "spending" money! Dressed in robes and turbans, he and his ten bodyguards didn't exactly fit in with the local dress code. His private 747, and five limos were on 24-hour call. Also on call was his own personal chef. But the chef never got a chance to rattle those pots and pans.

What does a sheik's nephew, and ten bodyguards eat while losing $2 million? McDonald's, what else. Every morning the maids found at least a dozen McDonald's wrappers in the five suites belonging to the sheik's nephew. He never used one restaurant comp for his entire stay."

Even a sheik deserves a break today.

Ask Larry

Larry King is to talk-radio what Charlie Parker was to jazz — an innovator, with a never-ending ear for conversation and improvisational ideas. Because of you, Larry, I was six months behind schedule in writing this book. Your radio show has succeeded where family and friends have failed. It gets me away from the typewriter. In his book, "Tell It To The King," Larry tells the ultimate win/lose story.

One night, Larry gets a call from a guy who sounds like he's jumping out of his skin with excitement. "Larry, Larry, I'm a degenerate gambler. This morning I was leaving the house and the wife says to me, 'Gamble once more and the marriage is over.' So I told her I was going on a business trip. Did you happen to notice the triple in the last race at Aqueduct?"

Larry told him he didn't have the paper in front of him.

"Go look it up. I'll wait," said the caller. "Twenty-nine thousand bucks, Larry. One ticket. You're talkin' to him. Wait a minute, there's more. I went to Atlantic City with the twenty-nine grand."

The caller paused for a moment then added, "Larry, I've got ninety-six thousand dollars in hundred-dollar bills. I'm looking at it as we speak. But the wife said if I ever gamble again, she's leavin' me. What do I do?"

Larry asked the caller if he wanted to break up the marriage. The caller said no. "I can only tell you what I'd do in the same situation," said Larry. "I'd be at the breakfast table when she came down in the morning, and I'd have the money under the table. I'd say, 'I broke our vow yesterday, I gotta admit to you, honey. I'm sorry,

I don't know what to say to you.' And then, I'd start peeling it off. One bill at a time.''

Slowly I Turn, Step By Step

I'm going to use an old Vaudeville routine to set up this story. The routine centers around a man searching for his wife. The wife ran off with the man's best friend. Traveling around the world, the man finally finds her in Niagara Falls. Now, every time someone mentions "Niagara Falls," the man flips out. Written by John Grant, and made famous by The Three Stooges, this classic piece of material has found its way into the slogan world of the '90s.

"Have A Nice Day" — annoying to hear and stupid to say, but like it or not, it's every salesperson's way of saying thank you. Some $100,000-a-year casino marketing "genius" came up with the new and improved casino version: "Have A *Lucky* Day."

Picture a casino gift shop at 4 a.m. A young woman working her way through college sits behind the counter reading a textbook. Her concentration is broken when a man enters the store. He's wearing a very expensive suit. His eyes, showing the battle scars of a long losing spree, glance over the magazines and newspapers. A New York Times in one hand, and a five-dollar bill in the other, the man walks over to the cash register. After ringing up the sale, the girl hands the man his change. Smiling she says, "Have a lucky day."

The man just stares into space for a minute. Almost in a whisper he repeats, "Have a lucky day?" Then a little louder, "Have a lucky day?!" Now screaming, "Have a lucky day, have a lucky day!"

Suddenly, things that aren't supposed to fly are flying. Postcards, souvenir sweatshirts, newspapers, anything that isn't nailed down. The man is trashing the gift shop. Picking up the phone, the girl calls security.

"The gift shop was a mess when we got there," said Jim, a security guard. "The guy was just standing there apologizing. He said, 'Call the casino host and tell him Mr. H. needs to see him.' A minute later, the casino host comes into the gift shop. It seems that Mr. H. lost over $150,000 that day, and when the girl said, 'Have a lucky day,' he went over the brink.

"The casino host told him not to worry and instructed me to escort Mr. H. to his room. So now me and Mr. H. are in the elevator going up to his suite. He's not saying a word. Everything is quiet except for the music playing in the elevator. The hotel runs its own promotional ads over the house P.A. system which cuts off the music.

"Suddenly, I hear, 'And for the best in late night dining try our coffee shop on the second floor. Open 24 hours for your convenience. And, have a lucky day!'"

Air Mail Special

"I've been cursed at, spit at, had drinks thrown at me, and smoke blown in my face," said a blackjack dealer. "The cursing doesn't bother me. You know the old saying, 'sticks and stones...'? The smoke, it comes with the territory. But when players start throwing stuff at me... hey, I didn't take this job to be some sore-losin' jerk's personal target.

"One night I'm dealing to a guy who's playing two hands, $2,000 a pop. Five shoes later, the player's losin' $50,000. By now, he's called me every name in the book, plus some I've never heard before, and I've heard them all. With blood pressure rising, his temperature boiling over, he signed another marker. It's times like this when I wish I'd read the fine print on my hospitalization plan.

"Pushing $25,000 in chips toward the player I said, 'Better luck sir.' Looking me straight in the eye without blinking the player said, 'Let's hope so, for *your* sake.'

"His first bet signalled the start of what I call, the 'Steeple Chase.' That's when a player starts chasin' his money. Three thousand a hand, and miles away from the home stretch. I'll never forget the hand that sent him over the edge. I've got a 6 showing. His first hand: two aces; his second hand: two tens. He split the aces and got a 9 on both. Three hands, $3,000 each, all totaling 20. I turn over my hole-card, which was a 2, giving me a total of 8. Four cards later, I've got 21. The player picks up a glass ashtray and throws it at me."

"Did they throw him out of the casino?" I asked.

"Are you kiddin'," said the dealer. "He signed another $50,000 marker and they put plastic ashtrays on the table."

Get The Lead Out

It's not unusual for a crowd to gather around a table to watch a high roller in action. Security guards, like bookends, rope off the area giving the player plenty of elbow room. Casino personnel cater to the player's every need. Nothing weird or unusual about this scene except for one thing: a janitor is also standing next to the security guards with his broom and dust-pan.

Stacks of black chips totaling $50,000 stand in front of the high-rolling roulette player. To his right is a box of new and recently sharpened pencils. The player bets five numbers straight-up, $100 each. As the dealer released the ball, the player would reach into the box for a pencil. Tapping nervously on the table, and turning his head away from the wheel, the player waited for the call.

"Seventeen," said the dealer as she placed the plastic tube on the winning number and swept the table clean of all losing bets.

The player, who always carried his own notebook would write down the number. Then, looking the dealer straight in the eye he would smile. His expression reminded me of actor Anthony Perkins playing Norman Bates in Psycho. He had that Norman pre-shower look in his eyes. The player would then snap the pencil in half and throw it into the air.

"That was *not* my lucky pencil," said the player as he reached into the box for another one. The janitor would sweep up the broken pencil as the player placed another $500 in bets. On the few occasions when the player won, the pencil's life was spared.

A few months later, I saw the same player with a cast on his pencil hand. Now, instead of snapping the pencils in half, the player would smash them using his cast. After a long and unsuccessful session, the player asked the pit boss to sign his cast. "Write something clever," said the player. The pit boss wrote the following: "Roses are red, violets are blue, at $500 a pencil, the casino loves you!"

22 Skiddoo

A musical group from Nebraska, performing at a local casino, will never forget their piano player's birthday. A sing-along version of "Happy Birthday" inspired someone in the audience to tip the band $25. The birthday girl, who just turned 22, was faced with a mathematical dilemma. How do you equally divide $25, six ways?

The bartender, besides being the underpaid house psychiatrist, had the mathematical answer. "You only turn 22 once in your life. Why don't you go over to the roulette table and bet the $25 on number 22?"

"You mean bet the *whole* $25 on one number?" asked the birthday girl after her last show.

"Let it all ride," said the bartender. "You're in Atlantic City now. This ain't no county fair in Nebraska. The carnival wheels here pay in cash!

"When you've been tending bar in a casino for ten years, you get x-ray vision. There are two kinds of smiles: a winning smile and a break-even smile. From 20 feet away I knew the birthday girl was a winner. She had a smile on her face bigger than any cornfield in Nebraska.

" 'We won, we won!' She kept repeating those words as she walked over to the bar." Her mathematical problem was solved. Eight hundred seventy-five dollars, divided seven ways comes out to a nice, round $125. Yes, seven ways. The bartender became an instant band member.

"Now, every time a new band comes in, I ask them if someone is celebrating a birthday. Hey, lightning can strike twice!"

CHAPTER 9

Blackjack, Then And Now

How do you get seven people to disagree? Have them all sit at the same blackjack table and watch them play everyone's hand. The game is certainly the most popular and at the same time the most controversial of all casino games.

History was made in Atlantic City when Ken Uston filed a claim against Resorts after being "barred" from the tables. Atlantic City casinos have since seen the immense popularity of the game grow year after year.

More books have been written about blackjack than any other casino game. Every author claims to be an expert. Readers claim superiority over the game after one hour of reading. And casinos make a fortune off these self-proclaimed superior experts.

Slot machines are said to be the "bread and butter" of a casino. Blackjack, in its current state, is the main entree. And there's no sign of anyone going on a diet.

Where did this alluring game get its start? Although the claims are conflicting, three countries — Italy, France and Spain — have taken credit for inventing the game. Two games from France, "vingt-un," and "trente et quarante," give the French reason to believe they started the game. The Spanish say blackjack is an adaptation of a game called "one and thirty." The game most similar to blackjack comes from Italy and is called "seven and a half." From this game, the term "busting" was born. If a player went over "seven and a half," they busted.

The game hit this country in the late 1800's. If history has taught us anything — and it always has — gambling, although illegal at that time, was never lacking for players. And players are always looking for a new game, new action!

To add excitement to the game, someone thought of paying a player three to two if their first two cards total 21. If a player was dealt the ace of spades and the jack of spades or clubs, the payoff was 10 to 1. It is from this rule that the game was baptized "blackjack." Through the years, blackjack tables have been baptized with gin, scotch, beer, and other casino holy water.

Some people get very religious when playing at the seven-seat altar. "We call her the flying nun," said a dealer. "She plays black chips and usually buys in for $5,000. Before she signals for a hit, she tilts her head back and looking up she'll say, 'God give me a five.' Or 'God give me a nine.' Halfway through the shoe she was down about $3,000 and decided to leave the table. Before she left her parting words were, 'God, I'm going over to the craps table because it's obvious that you're not in the mood to play blackjack today.' "

Casinos in Nevada starting dealing blackjack in 1931. The game always made money, for the house! Players and casino operators had no knowledge of the game. Basic strategy for the player bordered on the ridiculous: Rubbing a rabbit's foot on the table. Playing a hunch, or a gut feeling. But the "ice age" of blackjack would soon melt in the Nevada desert.

In 1957, the Journal of the American Statistical Association published a paper written by Baldwin, Maisel, McDermott and Cantey. This report was the first scientific study ever done on blackjack. From the results of this study, Roger Baldwin wrote a book called The Optimum Strategy in Blackjack. Scientists and mathematicians applauded Baldwin's findings. Casino personnel joked: "Just another system to sweeten the pot." They had no idea that the joke would soon be on them!

If I were writing a book about American history it would be impossible to omit Christopher Columbus. When writing about blackjack it would be sacrilegious not to mention Dr. Edward Thorp, a mathematician, who, like Columbus, made a discovery. A discovery that would change the course of blackjack. Casinos would panic and rules would be changed. They all laughed at Columbus when he said the world was round. Over four hundred years later they would laugh at Thorp. Columbus would laugh his way into history. Thorp would also laugh, all the way to the *bank*! Casinos don't like jokers!

A math professor from UCLA, Thorp wrote a book that would revolutionize the game of blackjack. Dr. Edward Thorp's bestseller, *Beat the Dealer*, published in 1962, became a blackjack player's "bible." And a casino owner's demon. Basic strategy, the ten commandments of blackjack, gave its apostles reason to believe. Judas would speak these words, "shuffle-up." A mathematician on a weekend trip to Vegas became the Walter Mitty of the gambling world.

Thorp, with the aid of computer expert Julian Braun, perfected a simple "card counting" technique. He wrote a paper detailing every step of the process. Published in the Proceedings of the National Academy of Sciences, it was considered to be "the greatest achievement in game theory since the sixteenth century." Girolamo Cardano, the gambler-mathematician, won acclaim in the 16th century when he did a study on the laws of probability and chance.

In 1965, Thorp left one casino and entered another, Wall Street. His firm, Princeton/Newport Partners, trades so actively on the New York Stock Exchange that it accounts for more than one percent of its total volume.

Thorp's blackjack career ended when a casino drugged a cup of coffee he was drinking. "I got drugged twice and then they banned me from playing."

Like two ships passing in the night, Edward Thorp and Kenneth Senzo Usui (better known as Ken Uston), sailed the same seas. The course of their lives was about to become a trade-off. The calm before the storm was on the horizon. Uston, a former stock broker and a senior vice president of the Pacific Stock Exchange, would chart a new course, a new life. Thorp, tired of the turbulence, went searching for the calmer seas. One was bored by the casinos; the other was lured to the casinos.

Resorts braced itself for the hurricane. The Atlantic City shoreline was about to be hit. The tide was about to change. Anchors up, the wind is blowing East. The invasion is about to take place. An SQS went out, the big *game* is in Atlantic City! The bait was too good to pass up. Card counters swallowed it hook, line, and sinker.

The bait was the favorable playing conditions here. Resorts was not allowed to bar counters. Early surrender, four-deck shoes, and a ruling by the CCC that required Resorts to deal two-thirds of the shoe. Ah... 1979, the good old days.

Card-counting teams from across the country came to Resorts. "They're coming out of the woodwork," said one pit boss, "Termites, that's what they are. They're eating up the foundation. They're killing us!" Termites? A building is falling? Murder? A little dramatic, don't you think? Another pit boss joked, "it looks like a card-counters' convention in here. If I see water-filled balloons flying around I'm going home."

Most of the "conventioneers" kept a low profile. But a few got carried away. Loud and boisterous, they were annoying the players, counters and non-counters. Gambling supervisors felt they were being ridiculed. "It's getting out of hand," said a supervisor, "They're jumping their bets from $25 to $1,000. A counter came to one of my tables about six hands into the shoe. 'What's the count?' he said. 'The running count or the true count?' asked his friend. They show no respect for me or my job."

Arriving in January, Ken Uston thought he would get a cold reception from the gambling supervisors. After years of being barred in Nevada, Ken was expecting the worst. In his book, *Million Dollar Blackjack*, Ken describes the atmosphere at Resorts. "I wore a disguise the first day I went to Resorts. I'd never seen a casino so crowded in my life. People were waiting in line for the 10 a.m. opening. After playing a few hours, shift manager Rick Howe recognized me and said hello. 'It's an honor to meet you,' he said, as he handed me his business card. I thought I was dreaming.' "

The dream would end soon but in the meantime Ken and the other counters would be allowed to play unhassled. Resorts had 70 blackjack tables and most supervisors feared a counter at every one. "It was like a three-ring circus," a former dealer said over a cup of coffee. "Counters were table-hopping; refusing to play against negative shoes. It was a floor show."

The floor supervisors weren't so amused. They felt the heat from upper management. The dealers felt the heat from the supervisors. A high-wire act without a net. But someone was about to fall.

"I was working day shift and the same team would play in my pit every afternoon. One guy said, 'How long has this candy store been open?' Candy store, can you believe that?" Having a sweet tooth caused their downfall. The team went broke after three weeks of play. Greed led to their decay.

Resorts knew there were counters among the thousands of players in the casino. Some were familiar faces from Nevada. Others went unrecognized. A physiological war was declared. The casino became the battleground. Resorts started the attack by restricting players betting $1,000 from playing more than one hand.

Phase two would be lowering the table maximum from $1,000 to $300. Only a handful of tables allowed $1,000 limits. The counters felt the tension mounting. B-Day (barring day) was around the corner.

Phase three: Resorts started dealing six-deck games at the $25 tables. The counters attacked verbally, "These six-deck games are great. We could win ten times as much with a high count!" Uston called this a "smokescreen," because the fewer decks dealt, the better for the player. The smoke went out the window. Resorts wanted to see the "white" of the counter's eyes. How do you trap a counter? Deal a two-deck game.

January 30, 1979: the war was over. Casino Control Commissioner Joseph Lordi gave the ruling that "counters" could be barred from playing blackjack. This brought a sigh of relief not only to Resorts, but also to Caesars which was due to open in six months.

Signs were posted on all blackjack tables stating:

> *"Professional card counters are prohibited from play at our blackjack tables."*

If a counter disregarded the posted sign, a casino representative would read the following statement to him:

> **"I represent the landlord of the premises. I am informing you that you are considered to be a professional card counter, and you are not allowed to gamble at any blackjack table in this casino. If you attempt to gamble at a blackjack table, you will be considered to be a disorderly person and will be evicted from the casino. If you are evicted from the casino and return, I will have you arrested for trespassing. If you refrain from gambling at a blackjack table, you are welcome to participate in any other game offered by the casino."**

Ah... do I have the right to remain silent and call my lawyer?

Boston attorney Morris Goldings and Ken Uston challenged the Casino Control Commission ruling. They fought against the legality of Atlantic City casinos preventing him from playing. Nine months after Uston filed his complaint, the CCC ruled that New Jersey casinos did have the right to bar counters based on common law. The CCC thought that it was unfair to bar "skillful" players.

The CCC finally came to its senses in 1982. It decided to make the rules tougher so that all players, skilled or non-skilled, counter or non-counter, would be allowed to play. Three rules were established:

> (1) The cut-card could be moved to halfway from the back of the shoe.
> (2) The house could shuffle the cards if the players tripled their previous bet at $25 tables and increased it five times at lower-limit tables.
> (3) The house could shuffle if a player joined a $25 game with a bet of $200 or more in the middle of the shoe, or with $100 at the lower-limit games.

Uston eventually was hired by Resorts as a "spokesman." Using disguises that once gave him access to the blackjack tables, he appeared in television commercials for Resorts. Surrender, anyone?

So, who are we to blame for all this confusion? The casinos, the counters, the CCC, the state? The finger points at no one and everyone. The casinos had very large investments to protect. Some counters "pigged out." The

CCC was trying to protect the state's revenue that comes from the gambling tables. Who really won?

Presently, 800 blackjack tables a day deal eight-deck shoes. That's 6,400 decks of cards every day, or 44,800 decks a week. How about 2,252,800 decks a year! So, I guess the card manufacturers won. Because of all the publicity surrounding the concept of card-counting, the game has become the most profitable.

"Twenty years ago seeing a woman at a blackjack table was unusual," said a pit boss at the Taj. "I believe that someday women players will outnumber men." He paused for a second and said, "I'll tell you something else. They're *damn* good players. Got nerves of steel."

I've become friendly with a man who's been in the gambling business over 30 years. He's a shift boss, and at his request I won't mention his name. Years ago, he dealt blackjack in New York and Ohio, in little "after hours" clubs. He went to Nevada in the '50s and worked as a dealer, floorman, and pit boss.

"John, what do you think would happen if we put 12 decks in a shoe?" A fair question. "The house would make more money and the tables would still be full." "What if we dealt one- and two-deck games?" "The house would still make money and the tables would be full." "You're right and I'll tell you why. The majority of the players don't know the first thing about this game. They have no respect for it."

Night after night, I've watched people approach a blackjack table as if they were buying a car or a refrigerator. First, they look at the price, the table minimum. Then they look at the salesmen, the dealer. Oh. . . he or she looks friendly, trustworthy, cute. Next they look at the customers, the players. Are they happy? If everything meets with their specifications, they buy in without looking at the product — the *shoe*. Are they buying a four-, six-, or eight-deck game? What they're buying is the *moment*, the *thrill*!

"Blackjack is like life," said one casino host. "Decisions, strategy, fate, but in the end we all bust. It's the in between that counts. Hopefully the victories surpass the losses."

Some players might have to live to be 100, just to outlive their losses! "I beat a player one night for $180,000," said a ten-year veteran dealer. "He really beat himself. One of the worst players I've seen. A player like that should stay home and *phone* the money in!"

Blackjack never loses its sense of humor. This classic story comes from Vegas:

A lady in her late 60s was heir to a very large fortune. Dressed elegantly, she and her friends would play blackjack. Dealers welcomed her because she was very generous with her tokes. A good customer, the sweet old lady never caused a problem.

But her friends, they were another story. Her friends were four stuffed animals. And like her, they also played blackjack. She would seat two friends to her right and two to her left. She sat in the middle. After betting $100 for each friend, she would order drinks for her thirsty playing partners. "Give Mr. Monkey and Mr. Kangaroo a beer, Bloody Marys for Mr. Elephant and Mr. Camel," she would say without a hint of embarrassment. She would also sample each drink.

Imagine the waitress telling her husband, "Boy I'm tired, I served a bunch of animals all night."

"I wish you could quit that job Doris. Those damn casinos are turning into zoos!"

Standing behind her at all times was her personal valet. After each friend was dealt a hand, she would signal for a hit. When one of her friends broke she would give it a slap, sending it across the casino floor. Her valet would pick up the busted uh... player and return it to its seat.

One night she had a $500 bet up for Mr. Monkey. He busted and she hit him so hard that his head fell off. Turning to her valet she said, "Bring Mr. Monkey up to the room. He's had too much to drink tonight." Only in a casino folks!

But how about the winning side? A dealer recalls a winning moment:

"The casino just opened. This guy buys in for $50. By the end of my shift he's up about $4,000. The next day he's waiting for my table to open. He could do no wrong and wins another $8,500. After three days of playing, he won $18,500. On a $50 buy in, can you believe that?"

Blackjack, a game of technical skills that has captured the heart and spirit of gamblers by the millions. A game that proves itself mathematically correct when played properly, and under the right conditions, but shows little or no tolerance for human error.

The plastic shoe demands respect from all those who seek its reward. The game continually puts our emotions to the test, from the five-dollar player who punches the table in frustration, to the $10,000 bettor who laughs at the game's superiority after losing a double-down.

So what's in the future for blackjack? Will the automatic shuffler take us one step further... backwards? Will dealers someday be replaced by robots? Is the machine age going to take the human contact out of the game completely? Is it that important to cut the shuffling time down to two minutes an hour? Playing nonstop blackjack could turn us all into zombies, and dealers into psychos! Dealers need that little break in the game so that they can deliver a one-liner back at the player.

Barney Vinson wrote two bestsellers: Las Vegas Behind The Tables, Parts I and II. Barney told the following story to publisher, John Gollehon:

A blackjack dealer had a rather hostile player at his table. Playing head to head, the $100 minimum game was taking its toll on the player. Every time the player lost a hand he would curse the dealer. Not loudly, but loud enough for the dealer to hear. This went on for six hours.

As the dealer was shuffling, the player stood up to stretch. During his seventh-inning stretch the player said: "I've been sitting too long, my ass fell asleep."

"I know," said the dealer, "I've been listening to it snore all day!"

I would like to dedicate this chapter to Ken Uston, my mentor, who died on September 19, 1987.

CHAPTER 10

If I Were A Rich Man

Jerry Bock and Sheldom Harnick wrote the award winning play, Fiddler On The Roof. Set in Czarist Russia during the eighteenth century, Tevye, a peasant farmer, dreams of becoming a rich man. "All day long I'd biddy biddy bum," sings Tevye as his fantasy of wealth turns rich in song.

There's a little bit of Tevye in all of us. Imagine flying to Paris for the weekend. Sailing around the world. Shopping on Rodeo Drive, where the word "sale" is a four-letter obscenity. "Oh, the good life," sings Tony Bennett, "to be free and explore the unknown."

Those brave souls called "high rollers," explore the unknown every night in Atlantic City. Thousand-dollar bettors searching for the hot table need no compass. The casinos will gladly lead them to the credit office. In Atlantic City, being rich is never having to ask: "Where are the $5 tables?"

Robin Leach has traveled around the world bringing us "The Lifestyles Of The Rich And Famous." If your idea of excitement is watching someone get a sun tan on the French Riviera, or skiing down a Swiss Alp, or eating some gourmet meal that's impossible to pronounce, then skip this chapter. But, if you want to read about a guy who nibbles on BLT's and monkey meat, and won $6.2 million in four hours, then read on.

So, Robin, if you're getting tired of being the world's most frequent flier, jet lag is getting you down, and your stomach can't take another airline meal, take heart. You can now rub elbows with the rich, 365 days a year in one location. The food is good (skip the monkey meat), and you're a jitney ride away from the action.

Need a place to stay? How about the $10,000 per-night Alexander the Great Suite at the Taj Mahal! That's where the high rollers rough it up when they're in town for the weekend. Atlantic City is a place where the rich try to get richer, and the rest of us try to break even. And all us Tevyes are "biddy biddy bummin'," behind the railing around the baccarat pit!

Edgar Allen Poe's classic horror story, *The Pit And The Pendulum*, took place in a dark and dirty dungeon. Swinging lower and lower, the pendulum slowly terrified the helpless victim. High-roller pits, with plush wall-to-wall carpeting, lavish decor, and million-dollar chandeliers have a built in pendulum called "the house edge."

The affluent players sitting at these $100 minimum games will sooner or later feel the razor-sharp blade of a losing hand cut into their million-dollar credit lines. Well, you know what they say: "A million dollars just ain't what it used to be."

For most of us, seeing someone lose our entire net worth on one hand is mind-boggling. "I guess you can get immune to anything," said Linda, a floorperson. "When I first started in this business, seeing someone lose $1,000 a hand was unbelievable to me. Now, there are nights when $10,000 bets don't even catch my attention. We once had five baccarat players from Brazil betting $50,000 a hand. Halfway through the shoe one of our regular customers sat down to play. Two hands later he left. He said his $500 bets made him feel cheap!"

You can't judge a book by its cover! And you can't judge high rollers by their clothes. "My $1,000 minimum table had a reserved sign posted," recalls Marie, a blackjack dealer. "I saw this elderly man dressed like a derelict walk into the pit. He had holes in his pants, and his shirt was dirty and wrinkled. Two security guards followed him as he sat down at my table. I thought they were going to ask him to leave. The pit boss and a casino host walked over to the man. 'Is everything all right Mr. B,' said the casino host, 'Are you comfortable in your suite?'

"For three days and nights, Mr. B played at my table wearing the same shirt and pants. His body odor was enough to make me want to vomit. After losing over $500,000, Mr. B checked out of the hotel. The clincher to this story is that Mr. B owns a chain of clothing stores for men!"

"We have a player who loves to draw attention to himself," said a pit boss. "We call him the 'egotist,' because he loves to play in front of an audience. He'll walk over to an empty $5 blackjack table and ask us to raise the minimum to $500. Playing two hands, a crowd is sure to gather and watch. The larger the crowd, the more he bets. Check that, the larger the crowd the more we win! The guy's a real showman. Why don't you interview him for your book?''

''I'm worth over 40 million dollars,'' said Mr. Egotist. ''I own a house in Palm Springs, a penthouse apartment in Manhattan, a condo in London, a yacht, and a jet. Every year I buy a new Rolls. Every suit I own comes from Bijan. I have the best that money can buy.''

I only had one question for Mr. Egotist. ''Why do you play on the casino floor, and not in the high-roller pit?''

''Listen, if you want to buy a piece of jewelry you go to Cartier's or Winston's. If you want to buy recognition, you make $1,000 bets at a table on the casino floor. Most people wouldn't know a real diamond if it bit them on the ass! But everyone knows a high roller when they see one.''

Maybe you're right, most of us can't tell the difference between a real diamond and a fake. But remember one thing Mr. Egotist, everyone knows a 24-carat ass when they see one!

As you can see, some high rollers have very erratic personalities. ''People think that I have a glamorous job,'' said one casino host as he tried to guzzle down a glass of milk for his Saturday-night ulcer. ''Some nights I feel like I'm working in a psychiatric ward. A player loses $200,000 and I pamper him, boost his ego, tell him there's always tomorrow, comp him to dinner, and a show. I pretend that I know what it feels like to lose $10,000 a hand.

"You lose all sense of reality in this job. My wife and I both work, and yet it always seems like we're just making ends meet. Tonight I got a call from a player who lost $250,000. The guy was complaining about the flowers in his room. He said the smell was giving him a headache! What am I, a doctor? 'Take two aspirin and go to bed!'

"The guy was looking for a little sympathy. I have all the lines memorized: 'I've never seen a dealer that hot before. The dumb shooter didn't hit the wall.' I bullshit them, they bullshit me. It's all bullshit.

"A player wins $200,000 and I still have to pamper them. Only now, I've got the casino manager breathing down my neck. Who the hell pampers *me*? It's a catch-22 situation. Without the high rollers I'm out of a job. *With* the high rollers, I'm going out of my mind!"

Depending on the player's status with the casino, there's no request too big or too small that won't be fulfilled. No matter how bizarre they might sound to you or me.

A player with a $500,000 credit-line loved to play two games, baccarat and Pac-Man. For the player's convenience, a Pac-Man game was installed in his suite. One year he lost over two million dollars at the tables. For Christmas, the casino had a Pac-Man game gift-wrapped and delivered to the player's house, in Portugal!

Another player loved blackjack and blondes. But not necessarily in that order. One night he wanted a pianist to come up to his suite and play something romantic. Two songs later, the player and his date walked into the bedroom and closed the door. Alone in the living room, the pianist was trying to think of a song to play. The blonde

returned to the living room looking for her cigarettes.
"What should I play?" asked the piano player.

"Do you know the Minute-Waltz?" said the blonde.

"Yes, I do."

"Well, play it twice and we'll both be home in time
to catch the Carson show."

A high roller once gave a casino host $1,000. "Go buy
a dress for my wife," said the craps player, "It's her
birthday and I can't leave the table. Her size? I don't
know, she's built like Jane Fonda."

That night the casino host asked the player — who was
now down $145,000 — if his wife liked the dress. "It
needed a few minor alterations, but she loves it. She's
wearing it tonight."

The dress shop's seamstress must have been a miracle
worker. The player's wife was built like Roseanne Barr.

Size 18, the hard way!

War has been declared in this casino town. A cold war
that makes the winter wind blowing off the Atlantic
Ocean feel like a summer breeze. There are no signs of
armistice, no truce on the horizon. Empty Dom Perignon bottles and half-eaten, five-pound lobsters litter the
battleground. Smoke rises from the earth, as the ashes
from a discarded $30 cigar slowly burn.

The field generals, wearing the uniforms of a casino
host, march to the front. Their battle plan is written in
a secret code. Mr. K.: $50,000, Mr. D. from Long Island:
$75,000, Mr. L., Mr. V.: secret weapons penciled in a
little black book. The action at the front line, better
known as the "credit line," is fierce. The longer the line,
the bigger the battle.

Prisoners are held captive in million-dollar suites. Wine 'em and dine 'em, but don't break them on their first night; let them suffer one loss at a time. Give them a victory once in awhile. Nothing too big, just something big enough to tell the boys back home.

If you see someone holding a white flag in one hand, and a filet mignon in the other, don't shoot. Chances are it's some high roller in need of a little R and R!

It's hunting season all year round for that endangered species called the high roller! And casinos from Atlantic City — not to mention Nevada — are all trigger-happy! Pass the ammo: Russian caviar and imported champagne. Don't fire until you see the green in their pockets!

"There used to be a joke floating around town when we first opened," said a retired pit boss. "The only high rollers at the Showboat are the ones upstairs bowling!" (The Showboat has a 60 lane championship bowling center above the casino.)

Today, the Showboat, and every other casino in town, have their own smorgasbord of high rollers.

In getting the material together for this chapter, I talked with numerous high rollers. Some didn't want to be bothered, others were just plain boring, and some couldn't speak English. Like a gambler waiting for the hot hand, perseverance finally paid off.

Three high rollers, all with completely different backgrounds, were kind enough to let me enter their world. Everything you're about to read about them is true. To protect their privacy, and at their requests, I will not mention the casinos where they play. Their initials have been changed, to protect their privacy.

High Rollers... Up Close And Personal

Friday night, 9 p.m., I'm waiting in the hotel lobby for Mr. & Mrs. B. to arrive. Mr. B. graduated with honors from Yale, and now heads his own company. Mrs. B. is a lawyer; her alma mater: Harvard. Last year, after expenses and taxes, Mr. and Mrs. B. netted $12 million. That's not counting their blue chip stock portfolio and real estate investments.

"We're not speculators," said Mr. B., "we invest for the long run." Those words kept going through my mind as I waited. I guess when you're netting $12 million a year, you can afford to run that extra mile. Long distance runners Monday through Friday, casino sprinters on the weekends!

Ten p.m. The check-in lines stretch across the main lobby. Outside, valet parking attendants jockey GM thoroughbreds down the home stretch. A white limo, weaving its way through the gridlock in front of the hotel, stops. A uniformed chauffeur, standing at attention, opens the back door. Emerging from the white chariot are Mr. and Mrs. B. They could easily pass as extras on the set of "Thirtysomething." Yuppies, with money and environmental consciousness, out for a weekend of spiritual enlightenment!

"I'm sorry we're late," said Mr. B., "but we were stuck in traffic."

I know what you mean. The Garden State Parkway can be murder on Friday nights!

"*Air* traffic," said a smiling Mrs. B., "We had to circle the airport for 20 minutes. My husband and I enjoy flying our own Lear jet!"

Mr. and Mrs. B. are only here five minutes, but the red carpet treatment is in full swing. A smiling casino host welcomes them. "Your suite is ready and I'll have the bellman take care of your luggage. If you need anything please call."

While the nickel-and-dime players stand in line waiting to check in, Mr. and Mrs. B. are being romanced by the casino host. Mr. B., feeling romantic, heads right for the casino.

Having never seen Mr. B. in action, I was expecting him to lead me right into the high-roller pit. Judging from the greeting Mr. B. received, I figured him to be a blackjack or baccarat player. We walked past the high-roller pit and through a maze of craps tables.

He's a craps shooter, I thought to myself. Hundred-dollar hardways, thousand-dollar come-bets. Wrong again. Mr. B. and I walked into the one area of the casino that I always try to avoid, the "premium" slot pit.

Mr. B. never has a problem waiting for someone to leave his favorite machine. There aren't too many $100-a-pull slot players standing around with coin buckets in their hands! Casino analysts call Mr. B. "the new breed of high rollers." Mr. B. bought $2,000 worth of $100 tokens and started to play, two tokens at a time. My enchantment with Ivy League schools began to crumble with every losing pull. A millionaire slot player wearing a Rolex watch, and loafers with no socks. Bugsy Siegel must be rolling over in his grave!

Two thousand dollars in tokens did little to weigh down Mr. B.'s coin bucket. "I'll just play with these tokens for now," said Mr. B., after another unsuccessful pull, "and then we'll go up to my suite for a drink."

Twenty minutes later I'm sipping a club soda in a three-room suite overlooking the Atlantic Ocean. Room service knocked and entered. Two bottles of Dom Perignon, compliments of the hotel. A large basket of fruit and three-dozen roses decorate the dining room table. Mrs. B. is busy making reservations: tennis at ten, lunch at one, massage, manicure and facial, dinner and show tickets. All first class and front row, all comped.

Mrs. B. is also a slot player... $25 machines. Hey, someone in the family has to know where to draw the line.

"Last year we had a total coin-in of $1.8 million," said Mr. B. The term 'coin-in' doesn't mean we lost $1.8 million, it means that we played that amount in action. My business is very demanding. Playing the slots helps me relax."

"These mini-vacations give my husband and me some *quality* time together."

Later that night, I watched Mr. & Mrs. B. spend some "quality" time together, relaxing! What is the going rate for "quality" time these days? Mr. B. went through $30,000 without blinking; Mrs. B. was down $7,500. One hour later, and three machines away, Mrs. B. hit a $5,000 jackpot. This little family outing really got interesting when Mr. B. hit a $10,000 jackpot. Now I understand why those jackpot bells ring so loud. They rattle something in the brain.

Mr. and Mrs. B., acting like a retired couple on Social Security after hitting a nickel-machine jackpot, were jumping up and down, yelling and screaming. Could this couple be giving me the bull? What the hell is $15,000 to *them*? They're worth millions! Ah... the thrill of victory makes us all, whether rich or poor, a little drunk with greed.

The casino host kept asking them if there was anything she could do for them. Mrs. B. wanted to see Dolly Parton, who was appearing at another hotel. "What night and how many tickets?" asked the host.

"Saturday night, six tickets," said Mrs. B., her eyes never leaving the machine. "No problem," said the casino host as she wrote down Mrs. B.'s request. The morning paper said that the Dolly Parton show was completely sold out. E.F. Hutton might talk, but $1.8 million in slot action screams!

I never realized how fast and non-stop the action is in the slot area. No waiting for a dealer to shuffle. No long delays over a misunderstanding at a craps table. Roulette has a slow, almost hypnotic rhythm. Mr. B., $200 a pull; Mrs. B., $50 a pull. In a little under five seconds the B.'s played $250 in action. At twelve pulls per minute, that's $3,000.

Around 3 a.m., Mrs. B. reminded her husband about their ten o'clock tennis match. Shaking hands, we parted and went our separate ways. If you're wondering how the B.'s did that night, let me sum it up this way: Six-love, six-love. Advantage: the Casino!

Everyday-wear for Mrs. G. is something by Bob Mackie or Chanel. Away from the tables, the soft-spoken Mrs. G. glows with charm and elegance. But at the tables, this five-foot three-inch jewel of a lady goes right for the jugular vein. Like a tiger in pursuit of her prey, Mrs. G., sensing a hot shoe, attacks. Her weapon, the poison dart that all casino owners fear: parlay, parlay, parlay... when the dealer's breakin', breakin', breakin'.

"You have to know when to go in for the kill," said Mrs. G., with a cold look in her eye. Tough talk for a lady who's over 70 years old and heir to a multi-million-dollar fortune.

"I only play blackjack and baccarat because I believe you can win if you're patient. Casinos are vulnerable to negative swings. It's up to the player to seize the moment. In life, patience is said to be a virtue. But at the tables, it's the calm before the storm. And I'm like a hurricane gathering strength with each winning bet!"

A poet and philosopher one minute, and a gambler with a sense of humor the next. Emily Dickinson and Aristotle, with a *million-dollar* credit-line! The sunken living room in her comped penthouse suite is breathtaking. A butler serves Mrs. G. and me espresso coffee and Italian pastries. Mrs. G.'s personal secretary enters the room: "Excuse me Mrs. G., Mr. G. just called. He's leaving New York now and should be here by five o'clock."

"My husband isn't a casino player, but he loves the horses," she told me.

"Is he a good handicapper?" I asked.

"He doesn't bet on them, he buys them! Would you like to join us for dinner tonight? Nothing formal, just the three of us. Do you like veal?"

At seven o'clock, with the sun casting dramatic shadows of the tall hotels, the view from Mrs. G.'s luxurious suite is captivating. Mr. G. reminds me of George Burns, not in looks, but in characteristics. "Did my wife tell you that we've been to every casino throughout the world?"

Mrs. G., wearing a beautiful and very elegant evening gown, enters the room. Her husband, with a sparkle in his eye, greets his wife. Hand in hand, they walk down the three steps leading into the living room. Love is forever young, regardless of what the calendar might say.

There are four gourmet restaurants in the hotel. But which one has Mrs. G. chosen for tonight? The butler answered my question in three words: "Dinner is served!"

If you can't lead a high roller to the gourmet restaurant, bring the gourmet restaurant to the high roller. Two rooms down from the living room is a dining room. Complete with Lenox china, Baccarat crystal, and table linens from Italy. Two weeks ago I was drinking grape juice out of a paper cup in the employees cafeteria 40 floors below the very spot where I'm sitting. But tonight, I have a butler pouring a cup of coffee for me and asking if everything was satisfactory. And my friends say I'm a starving writer!

"John," said Mrs. G., "let's go downstairs and have some fun." Mr. G. decides to take a walk on the Boardwalk.

"I always loved walking the boards," said Mr. G. "A cool ocean breeze, the array of people. It's funny, but the older you get the more you enjoy the simple things in life."

Mrs. G. took one step into the high-roller pit and all hell broke loose. Suits with badges came out of the woodwork. Pit bosses, casino hosts, floor persons, all converged around Mrs. G. The president of the United States doesn't receive this kind of welcome. But then again, the president isn't a $1,000-per-hand player.

Earlier that day, Mrs. G.'s secretary called the casino host requesting a $1,000 minimum blackjack table be reserved. The casino host, pit boss, and floor person escorted us to the empty table. A dealer unfolds her arms and begins to shuffle. Mrs G. is sitting directly in front of the dealer.

Like any red-blooded American gambler, Mrs G. does have her superstitions. No one is allowed to sit next to her. If a player wants to join the game, they will have to be seated two seats away. Two chairs are removed from the table, giving Mrs G. plenty of elbow room. Reserved signs, like bookends, are positioned on her right and left side to ward off the evil spirits. Try this at a $10 table and the pit boss will probably break a mirror, open a large umbrella, and have a black cat run a few laps around the table. Being a high roller does have its privileges.

Mrs. G. signs a marker for $50,000, orders a cup of tea, and lights a cigarette. She politely smiles at the dealer before inserting the yellow cut-card into the six-deck monster. "Good luck," said the dealer as she placed the cards in the shoe. "Thank you, dear," replied the table's only player. The cards are in place, a floor person is standing at attention. Mrs. G. is stacking orange chips ($1,000 each) into columns — $10,000 columns!

At the tables, Mrs. G. has the stamina of a 21-year-old. A head-to-head game moves quickly. The hand is quicker than the eye; $40,000 in chips vanish into thin air. Shoe after shoe, hand after hand, marker after marker, cards appear and disappear like magic. Mrs. G. plays flawless basic strategy, never losing her concentration. Her bets ranged from a low of $1,000, to a high of $10,000.

What two words, besides "early out," make a casino host smile?

"Marker, please." Without a quiver or sign of emotion, Mrs. G. signs her fourth $50,000 marker.

"Fifty-thousand," said the dealer. Her deep brown eyes are beginning to show signs of stress. The floor person has been by her side keeping a constant vigil on her every move. A pit boss gave her a look of displeasure when she incorrectly totaled a six-card hand. The eye in the sky never sleeps. Those 20 minute breaks do little to relieve the pressure.

"Fifty-thousand," echoes the floor person.

"Better luck, Mrs. G." The dealer's voice is soft and soothing. Her petite hands looked even smaller as they gently move $50,000 in chips across the table. Except for her wedding ring, the dealer's hands are bare. Ten years of shuffling and re-shuffling, and yet her hands remain soft, unscarred.

For those who stand behind the tables long enough, the scars run deep. Behind the eyes of every dealer there's a player, or a night, that just won't go away. The *real* players show compassion, understanding. Mrs. G. knows that it's not the dealer who decides a player's fate, it's fate itself!

Fate costs Mrs. G. another $30,000, but the player in her wasn't about to quit. At 4 a.m. and with $20,000 in her hands, Mrs. G. sat down at the baccarat table. Once again it became obvious to me how important it is for a casino to have a player like Mrs. G. A losing player at the table was using obscene language. A floor person walked over to the player saying: "Sir, there's a lady present. Please watch your language."

"And what if I don't?" said the player.

"If you don't," said the floor person, "I'll have security escort you out of the pit."

"What the hell is this joint, a church?" No one was laughing at the player's sarcastic joke.

At $1,000 a hand, Mrs. G. was the Pope of the casino. At $25 a hand, the foul-mouthed player was flirting with excommunication! Mrs. G. whispered to me: "He's a loser for letting his emotions get the best of him."

The third shoe gave Mrs. G. the chance to "seize" the moment. Baccarat players look for streaks, or patterns. Choppy shoes are disastrous — a player's worst nightmare. Mrs. G. played every hand like a sweet lullaby.

This was a "banker's" shoe, and Mrs. G. was taking out a large withdrawal. Orange chips seemed to be falling out of the sky. There was no time to stack them into neat $10,000 columns. The shoe ended with a streak of nine bank-hand winners.

The cursing player, who at this point had nothing to lose, left the table with a flurry of four-letter words.

Pushing her chips toward the dealer, Mrs. G. said, "I've had enough for one night." Mrs. G. looked fresher than anyone else at the table. "This is for the dealers." Five black chips went into the dealer's toke box. Earlier, at the blackjack table, Mrs. G. also toked the dealer $500.

"One-hundred and fifty-five thousand," said the dealer after counting Mrs. G's chips, twice. The crowd, which had gather by the pit to watch the action, started to disperse. We overheard one of the spectators saying: "Look at all the money that old lady won!" Mrs. G. looked at me and smiled. She held my hand and pulled me closer. "John," her voice was soft, like she was about to let me in on a big secret. "I lost $45,000 tonight. To me, it's like going out on a date with the casino, dutch treat. Only I got stuck with the tip!"

Writing a chapter about high rollers would not be complete — in fact, it would be sacrilegious — not to mention the creme de la creme of craps shooters from the Northeast. Metropolitanites, who were once the chiropractic backbone of Nevada casinos in the '50s and '60s, are now slowly fading away, disturbing nature's balance on the casino floor.

I'm talking about the two-fisted craps shooters, who chew half lit Cuban cigars. Guys who drink Johnnie Walker Black on the rocks, and call every cocktail waitress "sweetheart." These guys are big tippers, who throw $25 chips into "Sweetheart's" tray, like a package-plan vacationer throwing coins in a fountain. For luck, or for image? The "Sweethearts" never ask. Years of long-distance walking across the casino floor has calloused their inquisitive nature. A thank-you toke and a smile can't heal their sore feet or aching backs, but it helps pay the bills!

We're talking "action" players, who belly-up to the green linen craps table, like a family about to sit down to a Thanksgiving Day dinner. The in-laws are easy to recognize; they're the "don't" bettors. As the dice pass from shooter to shooter, these Pilgrims of casino gambling give thanks, until someone sevens-out!

Ever since the Camelot days of Vegas, craps shooters have hungered for two things: Sinatra, and heavyweight fights.

"When Frank used to work the Sands in Vegas," said a retired pit boss, "the drop at our craps tables quadrupled. Our best players came from the Northeast. We also noticed a big increase in quarter slot play. We couldn't understand why the slots were so busy. One night a casino host figured it out. J. Edgar Hoover must have sent half of the bureau here to spy on Frank's fans.''

On this cold winter night, the Boardwalk in front of Atlantic City's Convention Hall is bursting with energy and excitement. A large crowd slowly filters into the massive hall. Tonight is fight night, Tyson vs. Holmes. Ringside seats costing $500 are reserved for the casino heavyweights, action players with undisputed credit-lines. High rollers, clutching their status — comped tickets, are rubbing elbows with Hollywood celebrities tonight: Jack Nicholson, Kirk Douglas, Mickey Rourke, Barbra Streisand, Cheryl Tiegs.

These craps shooters are from the Bronx, Yonkers, Long Island, Queens, Manhattan, Brooklyn, Staten Island, Philadelphia, Jersey City, Newark. Geographical neighbors, craps-shooting brothers.

Michael Buffer, the ring announcer, introduces the many celebrities and politicians in attendance. They get a lukewarm reception — Polite applause, but not too enthusiastic. Only one name will bring this crowd to its feet. Everyone present will stand, out of honor and respect, for a man of courage and dignity. The announcer is pacing up and down the ring. He knows that the next announcement will create an avalanche of applause. A volcano of memories will erupt from the $100 balcony seats down to the main level.

His professional voice suddenly becomes emotional. He's about to set off a verbal nuclear bomb. "Ladies and gentlemen, the former three-time heavyweight champion of the world, Muhammad Ali, A... li!''

The applause drowns out the second "Ali." Heads turn, angling for position; everyone wants to see a part

of history... a champion, a hero, a living legend...
Sugar Ray Leonard, Frazier, Spinks, Hagler. Everyone's
eyes, glazed with emotions, focus on Ali. Cameras flash
rapidly, like machine-gun fire on a darkened battlefield.
Controlled bedlam ricochets off the iron and steel walls.

Climbing through the ropes, Ali enters what once was
his domain, his fortress. His eyes hide behind a pair of
dark sunglasses. Standing center ring, the aging Ali
smiles. Hands that once ruled the ring seem fragile as he
gently waves to his adoring fans. Tonight, the brutality
of the sport yields to a compassionate moment. The
toughest of men fight to hold back a tear. The bravest
of men concede.

Fathers, who remember hearing about Joe Louis, or
Marciano, will continue the tradition. Tomorrow morning, their sons will hear about Ali.

Mr. L., who promised to meet me after the fight, is
sitting four seats away from "The Greatest." Mr. L. is
also sitting within a one-mile radius of $500,000 — one-
hundred-thousand dollar credit-lines, in five casinos.

The casino floor is quiet. Dealers, standing behind
empty tables, stretch to relieve the tension in their backs.
Cocktail waitresses exchange paperback novels. Bands
play to empty seats. Bartenders read tomorrow's racing
form. Pit bosses, filled with anticipation and nervous
energy, sip stale coffee out of Styrofoam cups. Casino
managers pray for an early knockout!

It took "Iron Mike" four rounds to answer every
casino manager's prayer. Eyes closed, legs bent, Holmes
hit the canvas. In a strange but melancholic way, this was
a symbolic sign. One generation falling while another

rises. Craps shooters, who once floated like a butterfly and stung like a bee, are hitting the canvas. Whether champion or challenger, no one escapes without a few bruises.

Telephones in the pits started to ring. "It's over, it's over," said one floor person. Those two words seemed to echo throughout the casino. It took the casinos one second to knock out every five and ten-dollar game in the house.

The heavyweights of casino gambling, the who's who of the high rollers, will be entering the ring any second now. They'll be knocking themselves out at $100 minimum tables; breakin' a sweat over hard-ways and double-downs; stickin' and movin' in the baccarat pit; TKO'n the casino host over comps. If I only had money, I thought to myself. I could have been a contender!

Mr. L. and I talked on the phone twice, but never met face to face... until tonight. Sitting in our pre-arranged meeting spot, I heard a husky, rough-around-the-edges, New York voice, "Hey, kid, are you the writer?" The man asking the question had thick, black, curly hair, and wore a perfectly tailored suit. Nothing off the rack for this 74-year-old self-made millionaire.

"I gotta gang of stories for ya. See this hand?" Mr. L. held up his right hand. "One night this hand held the dice for almost one hour. I made over $150,000, just on my roll."

A bragger? A showoff? Nah, just another $1,000 pass-line bettor relating another war story to an injured infantryman. Mr. L. also revealed his battle scars. "I also lost over $200,000 while my wife and daughter sat front-row listening to Sinatra. I learned a very important lesson that night. You might wanna put that in your book."

"What's that, Mr. L., never stay at a cold table?"

"No," said a serious Mr. L. "Never miss a Sinatra show!"

Mr. L. had a warm friendly smile. And as he talked I couldn't help but think that I've met him before. But where? Years of working night clubs called "The Silhouette," "The My Way Lounge," "Joey's Lounge," "Louie's Lounge," "The Four Kings Lounge," "Tutti's Lounge." That's it, I thought to myself. I've met hundreds of Mr. L.'s, east side, west side, and all around the island of Manhattan. Guys who know that a winning night is only the eve of a losing night.

Turning to his friends, Mr. L. said, "This kid is gonna write about me in his book. Say hello to my friends: Toothpick, Joey Doughnuts, and my brother-in-law, Tankie."

Joey Doughnuts told me, even though I didn't ask, that he was self-employed. Working those red and black colored-schemed cocktail lounges taught me one very important lesson in human relations: When a guy named Joey Doughnuts tells you he's "self-employed," don't ask any more questions!

"It's time for me to take a shot." Those words flowed so evenly out of Mr. L.'s mouth. Like a guy telling his wife, "it's time to go to the office." Walking toward the craps tables, Mr. L. stopped to watch a blackjack game. "You gotta be nuts to play this game," said Mr. L., lighting a cigar. "The table's loaded with kamikaze pilots. Suicide players. Guys hitting 15's and 16's, when the dealer's showing a bust card. These guys can destroy a whole table, and then go eat a lobster dinner without feeling guilty."

Kamikaze casino hosts began bombarding Mr. L with complimentary kindness. "Is your suite O.K.? Are you comfortable? Do you need anything? My best to Mrs. L. What can I do for you? Did you enjoy the fight?" BAROOM! BOOM! BANG! Mr. L. is comp-shocked! And he hasn't made a bet yet.

Thousand-dollar pass-line bets, thousand-dollar come-bets, all with double odds, Mr. L. had $12,000 laying on the table in 20 seconds. In 25 seconds Mr. L. also *lost* $12,000. The dice went around the table from shooter to shooter. A pattern was being established: The point, a few numbers, and then seven-out, line away, pay the don'ts. Losing $32,000 at one table seemed to be Mr. L.'s signal to leave. "Let's go outside for some air," said Mr. L. as he threw a black chip on the table saying, "For the boys!"

"Win or lose, I always toke the dealers, if they've done their job. Hey, it's simple etiquette. It shows you've got class! If I make a big score, I toke them real good. You gotta be a good sport, win or lose. Hey, there ain't nobody standing outside these joints pulling you by the arm to get you in here!"

The cold winter air on the Boardwalk seemed to wake up the philosophical side of Mr. L. "I love the uncertainty of gambling. I've shot craps in alleys, abandoned warehouses, army barracks, after-hour clubs, Cuba, Vegas. From cold concrete floors with some guy holdin' a flashlight on the action, to glamorous casinos. It don't make a bit of difference to me. It's the action, the instant reward.

"Whaddaya say before? I'm the last of a dying breed? You're right. Real gamblers could care less if they're standing knee-high in horse shit or on some imported million-dollar carpet. When the dice are passin', any joint looks gorgeous. Those million-dollar chandeliers, the wall-to-wall carpeting, dealers wearing fancy outfits, it's a book cover, not the plot. If Atlantic City had gambling in the '50s — legal gambling — Vegas would still be a ghost town. Where else can you drop thirty-two-thou, buy a slice of pizza, and breathe in that fresh sea air?''

On to joint number two, I mean, casino number two. Casino personnel swarmed around Mr. L. ''Good to see you Mr. L. What can I get for you?'' Mr. L., Mr. L., there seemed to be an echo in the room.

''The last time I was here I won $56,000. The way these guys are jumping all over me you'd think I won a million. They're Mr. L.'n'me to death.''

''Well, you're a high roller Mr. L.,'' I said. ''They're just doing their job.''

''See that guy over there? The one bitin' his nails.'' The man Mr. L. was referring to was at the next table.

''I would never play at a table with him. He's a nervous wreck. He's gonna jinx the whole table. Look, he's got $25 on the pass-line, no odds, and he's sweatin'. Probably has a wife, a couple of kids, a mortgage, a car payment, mows the lawn every Saturday. That, my friend, is the foundation of all casinos. The guy can't win. He's playin' with scared money. Hey, put this in your book somewhere: scared money is losin' money. Remember that. Casinos eat up guys like him for an appetizer. The least they could do is buy the guy a steak. But they won't. Do you know why?''

''Why?''

'' 'Cause guys like me get the whole cow!''

Mr. L. ordered a scotch and milk. I guess he wasn't kidding about getting the *whole* cow! "I got an ulcer," said Mr. L. "The milk helps settle my stomach!"

By drink number two, Mr. L. was down $27,000. His stomach was very unsettled. But then, ever so slowly, the dice began to change. The new shooter made a pass, then another. Like a whistling tea kettle on an open flame, the shooter was sending out a signal. PARLAY! PRESS! SEND IT IN! LET IT RIDE!

"This guy," said Mr. L., his eyes looking at the shooter, "this guy is gonna bail me out. Look at his eyes. See that look of determination, confidence. The guy has guts. He's a craps shooter!"

Unlike most shooters who just throw and pray, this shooter had a style, a rhythm. You don't rush a hot roll, you savor it! He held the dice between his thumb and index finger. Never squeezing, never choking, giving them room to breathe. He knows how fragile that moment is just before releasing the dice. His hand extends over the table as if he were about to shake hands with someone. Shooter, I would like you to meet Fate. Fate, say hello to the Shooter.

Just before releasing the dice, you could hear that clicking sound that dice make before taking their involuntary flight. The dice arched high above the table, almost like a rainbow. "Winner six, and it came the hard way." The stickman's voice cuts through the roar of pass-line players.

The game is moving smoothly. Dealers, despite the heavy action, pay all bets without error. The table was running like a hand-made Swiss watch. Precision timing, all parts flowing. "The guy's an artist," said Mr. L., "and he's painting a masterpiece."

This flawless, perfectly tuned piece of human machinery was about to break down. One player, failing to see the beauty, the splendor of a hot hand, would break the shooter's stroke. The Picasso Mr. L. was admiring was in danger of becoming a paint-by-number nightmare.

"What the hell's the hold up?" Mr. L. asked.

For the first time in 30 minutes, the stickman was not moving the dice. A player standing at the opposite end of the table was upset. "I had a $5 hard six, and I was not paid!" The floorperson and the player are having a summit.

"Can you believe this? Can you believe this?" Mr. L. kept repeating those four words like someone watching Armstrong walk on the moon. "Can you believe that idiot? The jackass has $500 on the pass line and he's worried about a $45 payoff. Now you know why I got an ulcer!"

A black chip, like a guided missile, flew across the table and landed in front of the "jackass." Mr. L.'s aim was right on target. "Hey buddy," said the Jim Bowie of chip throwers. "Take the hundred and let's get the game movin'. In case you haven't noticed, there's a crap game going on here!"

"How about the change?" said the hard-six bettor.

"Give it to the boys!"

The dice quickly moved to the shooter.

"Having money don't mean nothin'," said Mr. L., "unless you know how to spend it!"

CHAPTER 11

The Warrior

Bodies press against the waist-high marble railing that surrounds the baccarat pit. Players, tired of drifting from table to table, stand behind the marbled altar. Security guards nervously scan the large crowd.

"What happened?" a lady wearing a "Slot Buster" tee-shirt asks. "Was there a fight? Somebody die? Is Donald Trump here?" Her voice raises an octave with every question.

"Nobody died," said the security guard. "There's just a little card game going on."

Just a "little" card game? I don't know what game the security guard was watching, but a hundred bleacher-seat fans and I were mesmerized by the action in the baccarat pit. A man betting $200,000 a hand and acting oblivious to the large crowd, sat posture-perfect, his chair flush against the lavish oblong table.

A gambler's architectural dream rose up from the table. Neatly stacked columns of orange thousand-dollar chips, and gray five-thousand dollar chips, rainbowed off the green felt table.

They call him "The Warrior." He makes every high roller I described in the preceding chapter seem like nickel and dime slot players. The 53-year-old Warrior dresses casually: a blue-striped shirt, and black slippers. He looks like a guy stepping off a bus with a ten-dollar coin voucher in one hand, and a five-dollar food voucher in the other.

He has a "yen" for BLT sandwiches, marinated monkey meat, and imported tea. In one hour, this man will wager more money than 100,000 average players combined — $14 million!

His real name is Akio Kashiwagi, and he's the world's highest roller. "He plays only for fun," said his aide Darryl Yong. Mr. Kashiwagi had a little "fun" recently at the Diamond Beach Casino in Darwin, Australia. After one week of fun, the Captain Kangaroo of baccarat hopped out of the country with $19 million in his pouch.

Very little is known about this mysterious Japanese player. He was born in a small town near Mount Fuji. His father was a carpenter. As a youth, Kashiwagi worked as a tour guide. He presently owns a company called Kashiwagi Shoji, a real estate and investment concern located in Tokyo. He lives in a huge house, affectionately nicknamed "Kashiwagi Palace." His assets are said to total well over $1 billion.

Rumor has it that Steve Wynn, chairman of the Mirage in Las Vegas, arranged Kashiwagi's first visit to Atlantic City's Trump Plaza. Others say that Donald Trump met Kashiwagi at a party in Japan, and invited him to the Plaza. Donald Trump rolled out — and vacuumed — the red carpet for Kashiwagi and his entourage of three. "I really don't know where the hell he comes from," said

Donald Trump, when reporters questioned him about his new house-guest.

Industry consultant, Al Glasgow, was hired by Trump to size up the Warrior. "He's a real Samurai," said Glasgow. "He craves a challenge. When he's taking a break, he'd just as soon sleep on a cot!"

After depositing $6 million at the Plaza's casino cage, the "Samurai" was escorted to his barracks: a three-bedroom, three-bath, penthouse suite overlooking the ocean, with chandeliers hanging over the bathtubs, two butlers, a sauna, a pianist, and a 24-hour chef at his call. In the living room sits a smiling $800,000 jade Buddha. After two days of play it was hard to tell who had the bigger smile: The Buddha, or Kashiwagi, a $6.2 million-dollar winner!

Will this create a sudden surge in Buddhism? Could a reported win of $6.2 million give Catholic, Jewish, and Protestant die-hard baccarat players a reason to denounce their religion? Will this mystical and ascetic religious faith of eastern Asia replace the card-squeezing, ego-greedy, finger-crossing, hunch-betting player? Hey, if you see a guy meditating and pulling in stacks of gray chips, take off your shoes, throw on a robe, and join in on the chant!

"He played the game, and he won," said Donald Trump.

Kashiwagi's $6.2 million win broke all records in Atlantic City. Several years prior to Kashiwagi's arrival, a roulette player reportedly won $3 million at Steve Wynn's Golden Nugget.

To give you an idea of the enormous impact a player like Kashiwagi has on a casino, think about this. The week prior to Kashiwagi's arrival, gamblers bought $15 million in chips at the Plaza's 117 gaming tables. Trump Plaza reported a win of $3 million. The following week, when Kashiwagi was in town, the Plaza reported more than $33 million in chips sold. Kashiwagi's win resulted in the casino losing $3.6 million for the week at their table games.

"It was an honor to have him with us," said Donald Trump. "He's coming back."

Three months later, Kashiwagi flew from London to New York on the supersonic Concord. A private jet, compliments of Trump Plaza, flew the high-rolling baccarat player from New York to Atlantic City.

Arriving at the Plaza, Kashiwagi went straight to the casino cage and deposited two checks: one for $6 million, and another for a modest $4 million. The $4 million check didn't meet with the Casino Control Commission standards and could not be accepted. So, Kashiwagi applied for, and received, a $6 million credit line from the Plaza.

Thirty-seven stories above the casino, the Warrior planned his attack. His $12 million army, dressed in gray camouflage, was only hours away from hitting the battlefield.

Trump, wearing the battle scars from Kashiwagi's 10-hour, $6.2 million win in February, wasn't looking forward to another "Purple Heart." Jess Marcum, a mathematician, and Al Glasgow were hired to help plan a strategy that would catch the Warrior off guard.

Their main objective was to lure the Warrior to the table for long periods of time. The size of the player's bets doesn't increase the casino's risk, according to Mr. Marcum. With the casino having a slight edge over the player, all that really matters is the length of time a player sits at the table. Pages and pages of Marcum's hand-written charts have shown that a player, after one hour, or 70 hands of play, has a 46% chance of winning. But, after 75 hours, or about 5,200 hands, the player's percentage falls to only a 15% chance of winning.

But how do you get a player like Kashiwagi to sit at the table for long periods of time? Make him an offer he can't refuse. A freeze-out, $12 million agreement was made between Kashiwagi and the Plaza. The game would continue until Kashiwagi either lost or won $12 million. The maximum bet would be $200,000. This wasn't going to be your friendly Friday night, winner-buys-the-pizza poker game.

Edward Tracy, president of casino operations, had this to say after presenting the idea to Kashiwagi: "His nostrils were wide open; he was hooked and going down."

"Hooked and going down," sounds like Tracy was talking about a fish. In casino jargon, a player who bets large sums of money is called a "Whale." Which leads us to the casino Biblical question. Would Kashiwagi, the Whale, turn Donald Trump into a modern-day Jonah?

After three days of play, the Whale showed no signs of going down. He was up $5.5 million. "It's hard to keep track of this kind of play," said David Coskey, a casino spokesman. "There can be million-dollar swings in a matter of minutes."

If you think Coskey's statement was an exaggeration, you're wrong. At one point Kashiwagi was losing $10 million; hours later he was winning $9.6 million. Almost $20 million exchanged hands, and the clock was still ticking!

Seconds, minutes, hours, the clock's hands moved closer to sounding the alarm. A peaceful, beautiful, $12-million dream would soon become a nightmare. But for whom?

I have 30 minutes to kill. At seven o'clock, four other musicians and I will be playing at a private party upstairs in one of the ballrooms. The party is for Trump Plaza employees, celebrating their fifth year with the Plaza.

But now it's that inbetween-time of day for the casino. Day-trippers board buses or chauffeur themselves home. The night-owls — showered, shaved, perfumed, and bankrolled — will be arriving within the hour.

Ten feet above the casino floor, from the steps leading to Jezebel's Lounge, I scan the casino. Like someone searching the newspaper for a headline, my eyes see the bold print of the casino's late edition: THE WARRIOR IS STILL HERE!

Like spring-fevered window shoppers strolling New York's Fifth Avenue, casino browsers gather around the baccarat pit. Their faces, pressed against the glass window, reflect mixed emotions of admiration and jealousy.

Callow players stare incredulously at the Warrior. Casino executives, frozen in posture like store-window mannequins, decorate the pit. Their icy eyes contemplating the Warrior's next move.

Scattered throughout the gallery are the "casino underdogs," players who charge into a casino with clenched-fist hundred-dollar bills and million-dollar dreams. Pockets empty, eyes filled with envy, they cheer for the Warrior. They stand shoulder to shoulder, like fraternity brothers.

That pandemic plague called "the casino edge" shows little or no remorse for the casino underdogs. Tomorrow morning they'll nurse their "I shoulda" hangovers. "I shoulda" quit while I was ahead. "I shoulda" quit when I was even. I shoulda, I shoulda!

The casino underdogs need a "folk hero." Someone who can bring the casino to its knees. Break the bank. Bust the joint. Give the casino a taste of its own medicine.

The gallery of underdogs are putting all their hopes and aspirations on the Warrior. He has the power, stamina, and guts. But most important of all, he has the *money*!

Casinos also believe in folk heros. They've seen a thousand Caseys at bat strike out with $500,000 markers glued to their hands like pine-tarred Louisville sluggers!

Hour after hour, night after night, in silence and solitude, I studied the Warrior. His facial expressions, like his $200,000 bets, never changed or wavered. The apathetic look in his eyes was constant. His nonchalant style of play awakened my curiosity. I read his mannerisms, using my instincts as a dictionary.

And then, like a misspelled word jumping off a page catching a reader by surprise, I saw the Warrior's linguistic flaw. A subliminal signal that con-artists call a "tell."

The dealers are waiting for the Warrior to throw in the Banker's hand. From where I'm standing, I have no idea what the Player's hand totals. I can't see the cards and the caller's voice is distant. The Warrior, now looking at the Banker's hand for the first time, gives off his "tell."

Tilting his head slightly to the right, his face showing no emotion, he throws the cards face down to the dealer.

I must have seen that little tilting motion a hundred times, never realizing until now what it meant. The Warrior "told" me he had a winning hand. The dealer, sliding $200,000 in chips toward the Warrior, told me I was right.

Last night, Kashiwagi was "telling" so much that there wasn't any room left on the table for him to stack his chips. What's a player to do? Simple. Just stack the gray $5,000 chips in columns of 20, and place them under the table. It makes a helluva hassock. But today, the only thing under the Warrior's slippered feet is the plushly carpeted floor of the baccarat pit.

Like a vulture sensing a helpless wounded animal, the casino's "edge" has begun circling its prey. The slow painstaking mathematical process of grinding a player down had started. No, the Fat Lady wasn't singing yet. But she was warming up!

A man who I know only by sight nods hello. I've seen him standing by the baccarat pit every night. I thread my way through the crowd and stand next to him. With his eyes glued to the table and talking out of the side of his mouth, he said, "The guy can't do nothin' right tonight. He lost eleven hands in a row. He dropped over $3 mill on this shoe alone."

His voice sounding like a racetrack junkie telling a latecomer the results of the daily double. The man offers no more information, but he repeats, "three-mill," three times. As the yellow cut-card comes up for air, the dealer announces, "last hand."

The Warrior slides 40 gray chips — $200,000 — across the table. He's betting bank. Two players who have been with the Warrior since day one are betting a bit more conservative — $50,000. I'm standing flush against the railing. This is the closest I've been to the Warrior. I'm right on top of the action. Ringside. It's Superbowl Sunday, and I'm on the 50-yard line. I've never been this close to so much money in my life. Over eight million dollars in chips lay on the table in front of the players.

A linen-covered, buffet-style table with tea pots, imported china, and warm towels nestles the wall. Shirt-and-tie executives, arms folded, legs tired, watch the battle against fate. Could the Warrior's coup de grace with fate be far away? "Cards please," the caller's voice was polite and clear.

The Warrior dealt one card to the Player, one to the Banker. Then another to the Player and another to the Banker.

"The players have eight and stand," said the caller.

The two cards representing the Banker's hand laid face down. Unlike the calm expression on the Warrior's face, his two friends are grinding their teeth. They look like they're in pain. One player, his fingers tapping nervous rhythms on the table's surface, never looked at the Warrior. The other player, with chips clicking in his right hand, kept his head down.

From where I'm standing, the Warrior and I are face to face. His eyes never blink, glancing over the cards laying in front of the dealer. This is a very important hand for the Warrior, and for the house. A psychological hand.

We have all faced a disastrous shoe, a cold craps table, a non-hitting machine, an uncooperative roulette ball. Players are broken in two ways: monetarily and psychologically. Then suddenly, when the end of the shoe gives us three blackjacks in a row, or that last quarter lines up the 7's, our confidence is quickly restored.

That last-ditch win embraces us in a world of unrequited love. Luck? Fate? Skill? Who knows? Who cares? It's a turning point. An answered prayer. An insulin shot for a diabetic bankroll. We're back in "action!"

In every casino there's a magnetic force called "hope." And everyone — players, owners, dealers — and yes, even the Warrior, are drawn into this metallic web of delirium.

The Warrior needs a winning hand. The choppy shoe has made him seasick with despair. He needs a dose of Dramamine. Something to straighten out the shoe's equilibrium.

The casino needs a losing hand. Yes, a losing hand. The casino's magnet is gripping tighter on the Warrior. And no one wants to see him slide off his chair, yet! Keep him glued to the table. Give him a seatbelt. Buckle up for the head-on collision with the casino edge.

Let him win a hand once in a while. Just to keep him interested and inspired. Throw him a bone. Lead him on. Then, very gently, start to break him, one shoe at a time.

I wonder if the executives standing in the pit understand a player's psyche? More importantly, are they thinking like "players" or "executives"?

"The players have eight and stand," the caller repeats himself like an actor giving his amnesic co-star a cue.

The drama begins as the Warrior slowly picks up the cards. He separates one card from the other. His eyes show nothing as he mentally totals the hand. Some players "tell" by tapping the shoe, or snapping the cards, when they realize they have a winning hand. The Warrior isn't a snap, crackle, or pop player.

I'm looking for the Warrior's tell, but there is none. Instead he smiles, almost on the verge of laughter, like he's just heard a joke. I'm confused, I've never seen him do this before. He seems jubilant. Then I realized, he just saw the punch line!

The cards seem to float out of the Warrior's right hand, as he tosses them to the dealer. Two cards glide over the table, like giant pieces of confetti tossed in celebration. The four-of-hearts, with one corner slightly bent, lands face up. Its flight companion misses the runway and crash-lands, face down. The dealer reaches across the table for the Mayday card.

"Bank wins, nine over eight," says the dealer as he taxis the five-of-clubs safely home.

Sipping a glass of ice water, the Warrior looks relaxed. His friends look relieved. As the dealers shuffle the eight new decks of cards, the Warrior rises from his seat. A cocktail waitress brings him a warm towel. He wipes his face like a surgeon after performing a life-threatening operation. The shoe's prognosis has been upgraded from critical to stable. Even the Warrior's vital signs look good. He has $7.5 million in front of him. He's still in "action!" Fate just threw the Warrior a bone!

"I'd like to personally congratulate everyone here tonight celebrating their fifth year with Trump Plaza. Your loyalty and dedication is what makes Trump Plaza number one in Atlantic City. Hope to see you all on your tenth anniversary. I would love to stay longer, but as you know, we have a player downstairs."

Showing a sense of humor as he addresses the anniversary employees, Edward Tracy stands at the podium. A youthful looking man, Tracy shows no sign of the stress or strain he's been under for the last few days. Enthusiastic applause echoes off the ballroom's walls as Tracy leaves the podium. There seems to be a genuine feeling of camaraderie throughout the room.

Walking past the elevated stage, Tracy waves hello to the band. Tracy's relaxed charisma could only mean one thing: Kashiwagi, a.k.a. the Warrior, a.k.a. the Whale, was in trouble.

The party over, my cymbals tucked in for the night, I ran down to the casino. If the casino was getting closer to harpooning the Whale, I wanted to see it.

It's 3 a.m. In another hour the casino will close. Players order a "casino nightcap," a parlay-pressin' run on the rocks, with a twist of luck. Dealers, waitresses, bartenders, supervisors, musicians, and security guards, all reach deep within themselves for that second wind to finish the last lap. The casino is strangely quite, almost eerie. Maybe that's why the dealers call it "the graveyard shift."

With chips totaling only $4 million, and looking apprehensive, the Whale waits for the dealers to shuffle the new shoe. For a moment our eyes lock. I smile as if to say, "hello." He shows no response. I'm not offended or insulted. How can you get mad at a man caught in the abyss of a losing streak?

The Whale, after six days of grueling non-stop 12-hour playing sessions, finally came up for air. After 70 hours of play, and over 5,000 hands, Kashiwagi threw in the towel. Those days and nights of million-dollar swings have left both player and casino exhausted. Losing approximately $10 million, the largest recorded loss in casino history, Kashiwagi headed for his suite.

"He surrendered because he didn't feel like he had enough bullets left," said one of Kashiwagi's representatives. The "bullets" his representative was referring to were the 416 $5,000 gray chips in Kashiwagi's holster.

Problems arose the following morning when Kashiwagi decided he wanted to play again. Low on ammunition and looking for that one lucky shot, Kashiwagi withdrew his $2 million from the hotel's safe deposit boxes. It was High Noon at Trump Plaza's O.K. Corral. It was Dodge City, with Miss Kitty brewin' tea, and Donald Trump telling Chester to get that monkey meat out of the kitchen!

Kashiwagi waited impatiently as the dealers shuffled the eight decks of cards. I gave myself a pat on the back for hanging around. Sometimes you have to trust your instincts and discard all the facts. My intuition forced me to return to the casino.

Gamblers are a mixture of simplicities and complexities. Some confuse logic with magic. Others treat luck as if it were a shadow. Some are like characters in a Ferber novel, romantic gamblers with no respect for the opposite side of the table. I had the Warrior pegged as a blood-and-guts player. A casino General Patton. Victory, no matter what the cost!

The cards were shuffled, cut, placed in the shoe, but never dealt. The confrontation between man and fate never took place. Instead of facing an expressionless shoe of uncertainty, Kashiwagi was forced to face reality.

Thirty-five floors above the casino, Kashiwagi came face to face with the enemy. Executives from the Plaza held a private meeting with Kashiwagi. The results of that meeting would start a verbal battle between Kashiwagi and Trump Plaza. Daniel Heneghan, staff writer for the

Atlantic City Press, became an overnight war correspondent.

Kashiwagi, speaking to the Press through an interpreter said, "I was informed that they decided they did not want to carry on the game. Trump and his officials are dishonorable."

Kashiwagi filed a written complaint with the Casino Control Commission. He said that Donald Trump and the Plaza reneged on their $12 million "winner take all," handshake agreement. In a rather grouchy tone of voice Kashiwagi left the hotel, threatening to burn his autographed copy of Trump's "The Art of the Deal."

"He never really met his end of the agreement," said Edward Tracy. The agreement according to Tracy was for Kashiwagi to arrive at the Plaza with $10 million in cash and the casino would give him an additional $6 million in credit. But Kashiwagi supposedly came up $4 million short in the cash department.

"I informed him," said Tracy, "that we had accepted his decision to stop playing, but we would make every arrangement for him to go to Trump's Taj Mahal, if he could obtain more fresh cash."

Tracy told Kashiwagi that if he wired six "fresh million dollars" to the Taj, he would be allowed to bet $150,000 a hand. If he wanted to bet $200,000 a hand, he would have to wire $8 million to the casino.

Kashiwagi refused Tracy's offer saying, "They don't honor what they promise." Dejected and defeated, Kashiwagi kept insisting that he be allowed to play at the Plaza.

Describing Kashiwagi as a shrewd and worthy opponent, Tracy stood firm on the Plaza's decision. He called

Kashiwagi a "sore loser" who was trying to put pressure on the Plaza through the Casino Control Commission. A very angry Warrior left the hotel vowing never to play at the Plaza again.

Get in line, Kashiwagi. There's a million "vow" breakers walking around the casino looking for a little ecclesiastical clemency!

Tracy, in responding to Kashiwagi's arrogant rage, said, "We weren't real happy when we lost $6 million in February and paid him instantly."

Adding insult to injury, Kashiwagi said he will never forgive the indignities he suffered. According to Mr. Yong, Kashiwagi's aide, Donald Trump arranged a $5,000 credit at Macy's for Kashiwagi. But — and this is Yong's side of the story — the credit proved worthless. His purchases left sitting on the counter, Kashiwagi left the store in humiliation.

First of all — and this is by no means a reflection on Macy's — why the hell would a guy worth over $1 billion, and betting $200,000 a hand, go shopping in a mall? It's like Jackie Onassis sitting home at 3 a.m. eating a box of cookies and calling the Home Shopping Network to buy a dress!

Trump officials made a phone call and Macy's delivered everything to Kashiwagi's suite. "Not good enough," said Yong. "We pity Mr. Trump's creditors. No wonder if they panic."

Kashiwagi took a little stroll on the Boardwalk to Caesars. His most expensive piece of luggage: a $4 million check tucked deep in his pocket. The same check that the Casino Control Commission found unacceptable, was burning a hole in Kashiwagi's pocket. Caesars refused to accept his check, but they provided him with several suites for the night.

The following afternoon two limousines drove Kashiwagi and his party to the airport. A helicopter provided by Caesars flew him to an undisclosed location. "Kashiwagi's new hobby," said Yong, "will be golf."

The world's highest roller left Atlantic City without fanfare. The last "comp" for Kashiwagi was a free ride out of town. In a strange and peculiar way, it's a sad ending. For six days he held the casino world hostage. Owners, players, dealers, and casino voyeurs watched with inquisitive eyes. Dante's "Divine Comedy" staged in a casino.

The song may have ended, but the melody will linger in casino concert halls throughout the world. Kashiwagi, the green-felt Pied Piper, no longer owns the flute!

The name "Kashiwagi" will live forever in the cold dusty archives of the casino world. A legend in his own time. An author who was one chapter away from a masterpiece. A player who was one step away from breaking the bank. I guess we can all learn a lesson from the Warrior: When the shoe doesn't fit, take a walk.

I'd like to add my own personal thoughts on the Warrior vs. the casino. It's probably the first time I've ever seen two "sore winners." The mudslinging and finger-pointing can't hide the truth. Kashiwagi won $20 million in Australia and $6 million at the Plaza. That's $26 million! Then, he lost $10 million back to the Plaza. Hey, Kashiwagi, what's the problem? You're still ahead $16 million!

After the dust settled in the baccarat pit at the Plaza, not only did they get their $6 million back. They *won* $4 million. Wouldn't we all like to be "sore winners," just once in our lives?

Rolled up and tucked away, the red carpet awaits the next Whale. Somewhere, someplace, there's an insomniac gambler pacing the casino floor looking for an edge... a new angle. A failsafe system to beat the house... the odds. The casino's welcome mat awaits all those brave new challengers. Remember one thing, the casino isn't the enemy. The allies standing behind the tables are doves. The real enemy is fate. The real ally is luck.

CHAPTER 12

Lucky Stars

Reflections, Harrah's 24-hour restaurant comes alive at 4 a.m. Players console each other over coffee. Casino stories pass from table to table like freshly baked pastries. You can always tell who the winners are. They're the ones ordering banana splits before they've finished their steak and eggs. The veterans of casino warfare stagger in with the Daily News tucked under their arms, the Purple Heart of the "break-even" crowd.

Losers, they're easy to spot. Sometimes they hold the menu upside down. The look of indecision bounces off the smooth, glossy surface of the plastic menu. Chained, designer-frame bifocals hang below the chin. The unchained ones sit on foreheads or nest in receding hairlines. Then the verbal give-away:

"May I take your order?"

"I'll just have coffee."

"Decaf or regular?"

"Ah... make that a cup of tea."

"Lemon or cream?"

"Ah... can I just have a glass of water?"

"Tap or bottled?"

"Waitress, you don't understand. I was ahead $500 until this midget-brain idiot sat down... splitting tens, hitting hard 17's. God, it was horrible."

"How 'bout a nice cup of hot chocolate?"

"Yeah. Sure. A hot chocolate... with lemon!"

I was sitting at the counter reading a book about astrology. A man sitting two seats away eyed the cover. He asked, "Do you believe in using your zodiac sign at the tables?"

I thought he was joking so I said, "No. But if they ever open a casino called Your Lucky Stars, I might consider the idea."

"I was never a superstitious type of guy," he said. "I always thought that skill and knowledge were a player's best allies. Plus a little luck. Show me an unlucky skilled player and I'll show you a loser!"

Stirring his cup of coffee he said, "Three months ago I was on a losing streak. It ended one night with a $50 buy-in at a craps table. When I left the table I had green and black chips totaling $650 in my pocket.

"Before I went to sleep I read the newspaper. I never read the horoscope section. But that night something made me turn the page. My horoscope read, 'Your luck will run smoothly today. Big gains await you.'

"Isn't that weird? There I was sitting at the kitchen table with six hundred and fifty big gains staring me in the face."

Staring *him* in the face I said, "It was probably just a coincidence. A fluke!"

"That's what I thought. But then it happened again. I made a $500 score four nights later. Out of curiosity

I turned to the horoscope section. 'Money will reward your actions today!'

"I couldn't sleep that night just thinking about what had happened. I was debating with myself about how I was going to spend the $1,100. Put eight in the bank and give my wife the rest? Pay off my credit card balance? Double up on my car payments? Put it all in the bank?

"Then it hit me. Instead of reading my horoscope at night I decided to read it in the morning. I had a so-called galaxy system working for me. If my horoscope had a positive message, I was off to the casino.

"About a week later my horoscope read, 'Today all your financial decisions will be... resolved.'"

There was a long pause after the word, "resolved."

"So what happened?" I asked.

"My horoscope was right," said the Age of Aquarius. "I didn't have to worry about making any more financial decisions. I lost the $1,100 in 30 minutes!"

That short conversation gave me the idea for this chapter. Have you ever experienced the following? You're walking through the casino passing table after table, machine after machine. There's a claustrophobic hundred-dollar bill in your pocket screaming for air! Then, for some strange and unknown reason something draws you to a particular table or machine. Echoing through the unexplored subconscious valley of your mind a voice is crying out, "Play here, play here."

Could this be a hypnotic suggestion from "Lady Luck"? Or is Benjamin Franklin doing a ventriloquist act in your pocket?

Some players call it "instincts," or a "gut feeling." That casino ulcer attack causes a player to double over the green-felt operating table without a sedative. "Play here, play here" — it's like a dull headache that won't go away.

All right, so we give in to the little voice. Suddenly you're the Houdini of the casino floor. Hocus-pocus, abracadabra, you're disappearing to the casino cage. It takes two hands to hold your winnings. Overweight coin buckets are bulging with the overflow of good fortune. You never won so much money in your life. But what really drew you to that table or machine?

Was it ESP? Karma? Did your instincts guide you there? Were you under the influence of a clairvoyant spell? Did you suddenly come down with a 24-hour case of "psychic powers"? Or was it simply "dumb luck"?

"We must believe in luck," said Jean Cocteau. "For how else can we explain the success of those we don't like?"

People believe in anything and everything when they're winners! Could there be a new wave of mystical players attacking the casino's crystal ball? Could the Edward Thorpes and Nick the Greeks of the 21st century be some star-gazing astrologers? Can Jean Dixon and Linda Goodman find love, happiness, and wealth at a blackjack table?

Can a psychokinetic craps player throw an unlimited number of passes? Are zodiac signs and horoscope predictions the casino player's racing form? Imagine a day when players will no longer ask a dealer, "Are you hot?" But instead ask, "What's your sign?" Is splitting tens, and doubling-down on hard twelve acceptable if you're a Libra, and the dealer's a Capricorn?

Could Zen, transcendental meditation, spiritualistic manifestations, and piped in sitar music become the casino ambience in the nineties? Will a dry martini or scotch on the rocks be replaced by some voodoo concoction?

Hey, if the guy sitting next to you smells like an onion, and he's raking in chips, don't offer him a Binaca blast. Run to the nearest produce stand!

Imagine people baptizing a slot machine with some homemade "magic potion" instead of a half-filled plastic cup of warm beer.

Is there really such a thing as "mind over matter" on the casino floor? Are players so insecure that they really believe in all this mumbo-jumbo? Let's find out.

> *"Advice is what we ask for when we already know the answer but wish we didn't."*
>
> Anonymous.

Horse Sense

Handicappers looking for that needle-in-the-haystack winner, study the small, black and white racing form. Speed, weight, class, latest workouts, and track conditions are calculated. Inside information better known as "tips," pollutes the clubhouse air causing handicappers to choke on their own insecurities. Logic, knowledge, experience, and rumors are all the ingredients these clubhouse chemists need to discover their wonder drug — the penicillin that cures every loser's ailment — a 10 to 1 non-program pick, I-told-you-so winner!

Let the suckers bet their lucky numbers, favorite colors, and cute-named horses. But if a guy comes along claiming that "Tu Vi" can beat the horses, don't scratch him out. He might be the longshot hugging the rail charging down the backstretch!

Nhat Nguyen, a Vietnamese refugee, has an unique style of handicapping. He spends five minutes studying the racing program. Then his eyes probe the galaxy of stars that embellish the dark sky. As the horses were cantering down the backstretch between races Nguyen's eyes came back to earth. "That one," said Nguyen as the horses pass the clubhouse.

The horse Nguyen singled out was Jim's Angel. To the handicapping crowd at West Virginia's Charles Town Turf Club, Jim's Angel, on paper, didn't stand a chance.

When asked why he picked Jim's Angel, Nguyen replied, "He has to be the one because he's standing in the east and his color is orange. The time is right!"

Handicappers understand a drop in class or weight. But a horse standing in the east? Hey, pal, it's your money. Bet the orange-colored nag if you want.

A few minutes later the time was right. Four lengths in front of the field, Jim's Angel paced across the finish line. The handicappers just witnessed a $12.60, East of Eden, orange-colored, Tu Vi winner!

Some inquisitive horse players asked Nguyen, "Why did you pick that horse?" But the smart ones asked, "Who do you like in the next race?"

Nhat Nguyen is a student of "Tu Vi," an ancient Vietnamese horoscope science. As a master of Tu Vi, Nguyen claims he has the ability to tell fortunes, offer sound advice, and soothe emotional upsets.

Nguyen entered a contest conducted by the Washington Post. Contestants were asked to handicap each race.

To win, all you had to do was pick more winning horses than your opponents. The winner of the contest would become the new harness-racing handicapper for the Washington Post.

Nguyen accepted the challenge but made it clear that the date wasn't a favorable one. After 12 years of studying Tu Vi, Nguyen knew that Saturday night was the Day of the Snake. Nguyen was born in 1940, the Year of the Dragon. Add these two facts together and in the language of Tu Vi, it's a poor omen. Even the time of day was against Nguyen's Tu Vi theory. He would only be "hot" between 8 and 10 p.m. The race-track Cinderella looking for a two-dollar win ticket was in trouble!

Nguyen's Tu Vi powers began to dwindle after the fourth race. After losing three races in a row someone asked him what went wrong. "I have no idea," said Nguyen. "There is a reason, but I don't know what it is." The aspiring Post handicapper added, "I don't believe in luck."

Ten p.m., and Nguyen was out of his Tu Vi time zone. Down $29 for the night he agreed to stay for one more race. "Plenty Color, in the eighth," said Nguyen. "I like him because his color is green and that has the same symbol as the time of day!"

Nguyen asked for directions to the men's room and left the table. The men's room was upstairs. Nguyen went downstairs.

As the horses hit the backstretch, Plenty Color — poised for the stretch run — went three-wide. Passing horse after horse, Plenty Color won by six lengths. Reaching into his pocket, Nguyen asked, "How much I win?"

Twenty dollars worth of winning tickets hit the table as Nguyen asked again, "How much I win?"

"Ninety-three dollars," said a bewildered doubter of Tu Vi.

"All I do is use my eyes and my brain," said Nguyen. "My eyes, my brain, and what I know from my country."

I wonder who taught Nguyen the old, "Where's the bathroom" trick?

Ask 100 people if they're superstitious and 99 will say no. If that's true, then why are there so many three-legged rabbits limping around — jade rings, lucky charms, four-leaf clovers, lucky pennies, lucky socks, wearing something red? It's everyday wear for the insecure, never-enter-a-casino-without-it player! Technology won't make those dice pass, or kiss that king-of-hearts with an ace. But those "thingamajigs" collecting mildew in the corner of your wallet put your mind at ease. It's the negative thinker's security blanket for those cold casino games.

Pass The Salt

"There's nothing worse than a winning, loud-mouth, superstitious player," said a pit boss. "I remember a baccarat player who sprinkled salt on the table everytime he won a hand. The guy would bet $3,000 a hand, sometimes more if he was winning. I felt like a waiter filling up salt shakers all night. When he was losing he was a pain in the ass. He would say things to taunt me and the dealers. Little dumb things like, 'Come on guys, pass the salt. The recipe calls for a dash of salt.'

He was an obnoxious player even when he was winning. He had these sly little cliches: 'Am I getting too salty for you?' Or he would rub the table saying, 'Hurts when I rub the salt into the wound!'

"We always had to have someone come down and vacuum the table after he left. One night after losing $60,000, he waved me over to his chair. He was sprinkling salt into his hand and tasting it.

" 'What the hell kind of salt is this? Here, taste it!'

" 'It's salt,' I said. 'Salt is salt. It's just regular salt.'

" 'Is this salt iodized?' he asked.

" 'How the hell should I know. I'm a pit boss not the Galloping Gourmet!'

" 'You don't understand. It's the iodide. The luck is in the iodide!' "

Don't "Press" Your Luck

"I've seen my share of superstitious players," said a dealer. "I remember this nutty guy, a real wacko — a craps shooter on a helluva winning streak. Three nights in a row this guy was beating our brains out. Winning big time. Catching one hot roll after another. Pressin', and then coming off just at the right time. Parlaying ten-dollar hardways and catching them. Hittin' $25 yo's.

"Every night he wore the same jacket. An ugly, polyester, multi-colored, one-size-too-big sportjacket. He called it his lucky jacket.

"His winning streak, like all winning streaks came to an end on the fourth night. He gave back all his winnings. So he started signing marker after marker. He reached into his pocket for a cigarette lighter and pulled out this little tab — a little numbered tag that dry cleaners put in your clothes. His wife was standing a few feet away and he called her over.

"Pushing the tab in her face he said, 'What the hell is this?'

"Looking at the tab his wife said, 'You've been wearing that jacket for almost a week so I sent it out to the cleaners.'

"He threw the tab on the floor saying, 'Are you nuts? Do you know what you did? How could you be so stupid?'

"She said, 'What the hell are you talkin' about? What did I do?'

"Shaking his head he said, 'I'll tell you what you did. You had my luck cleaned and pressed right out of my jacket!' "

My Left Or Your Left

"I always seem to get all the nuts on my shift," said a cocktail waitress. "A junket was in town with all high-rolling craps players. One player had this weird superstition. He told the pit boss that if a cocktail waitress served him on his right side, he would call off all his bets. The pit boss told me to be careful and always serve the player on his left side.

"Five hours, and I don't know how many drinks later, the player changed his spot at the table. I approached him on the wrong side and he got mad. Screaming he said, 'Take me down. I'm off. All my bets are off! Get me out of here!!'

"If looks could kill then I must have nine lives. The player, pit boss, and floor person gave me a look that I'll never forget. I figured that tomorrow I'd be working the nickel slots.

"Little did I know that I had just saved the casino about $40,000. It seems that when the player took his bets down he missed the hottest roll of the night!"

Jack In The Box

A lady dressed entirely in black and carrying a large pocketbook slowly climbed the stairs leading to the high-roller pit. Her face hid behind the black veil attached to her hat. Black, elbow-length gloves covered her arms. She wore expensive rings over her gloved fingers. Eerie, yet glamorous in a theatrical sense. For some reason she reminded me of Bette Davis.

Sitting at the empty $100 minimum blackjack table, she asked for a marker. Pushing the veil away from her face, she requested black chips. She looked dignified, but somber. Her gloved hand disappeared into the elbow-high depths of her pocketbook. A casino host greeted her, "So nice to see you Mrs. D. Where's Mr. D.?"

As her hand continued to Braille-search her purse she said, "Jack's right here!"

She removed a small box from her purse and placed it next to her. "Here's Jack!"

The casino host and the dealer turned a whiter shade of pale as they stared at the box of ashes. At a recent seance, Mrs. D. claims that Jack spoke to her: "Bring me to Atlantic City, exactly three months after my death, and your luck will be prosperous!"

Would this night make Jack the supreme "eye in the sky?"

Three hours later, and dressed for the occasion, Mrs. D. was attending another funeral — her own. She cremated four markers — $20,000. The grief-stricken

Mrs. D. reached for the box. Perhaps her late husband's ashes would console her in some way.

"Jack, you son-of-a-bitch," she screamed as she threw the box across the casino floor. "Death hasn't changed you. You're still full of bullshit!"

Acting whimsical or outlandish won't get you barred from a casino. But if you're a normal person who happens to be highly intelligent, and you're known around the world as a "mentalist," beware!

Truly Amazing

"I had a very bizarre experience one night," said the man sitting across from me. His soft, articulate, energetic voice circled the dimly lit room. A small table balances a decorative tray of assorted cheese, fruit, and crackers. Bottled water and soft drinks surround the plastic covered tray.

"In fact," he continued, "it was a very uncomfortable incident. I was sitting at a blackjack table making small bets. Six men walked into the pit and had a short, private conversation with the pit boss. One man, who reminded me of Brando in the Godfather, walked over to me. Standing next to me he said, 'Are you Kreskin?'

"I said, 'yes.'

"Looking at me, he said, 'Because of what you do, we don't want you to approach any game in this casino any closer than ten feet from the table!' "

Kreskin is not a professional card counter. He's been labeled everything from a psychic, fortune teller, a guru of the paranormal, and a clairvoyant showman. Kreskin has denounced these claims saying, "I'm not a psychic, I cannot foretell the future. I'm a mentalist!"

Skeptics, possibly jealous of his controversial mental abilities, have tried to discredit him. Believers in parapsychology are astonished by his unyielding proficiency. The general public is simply "amazed" by his brilliance.

The pit bosses at the MGM who came up with the ten-foot ruling were not amazed, astonished, bewitched, or bewildered. But they were intimidated. So what do you do with a mentalist who's ahead 82 memorable dollars? You ask him for his autograph and bar him from playing. But if he's losing, give him the old standby ESP comp — the "Everyday Sucker Perk" — a free meal in the coffee shop!

After his second show at Harrah's Bay Cabaret, I met Kreskin in his dressing room. I wanted to find out if Kreskin's expertise in parapsychology really gave him an edge over the casino.

"The truth of the matter is that I really have no advantage in spite of my work as a mentalist. I deal with people thinking and their concentration. My work is more related to how people think and their social behavior. Let me give you an example of what I mean:

"In Nevada, some blackjack games are dealt face down. The dealer only looks at his hole card in certain situations. You also have other players at the table looking at their cards. So if someone could read everyone's thoughts at the table, you wouldn't know whose thoughts you were reading!"

Most of us know Kreskin, "the performer." Some might say that he's a flamboyant entertainer playing "mind games" with the audience. But there's another side to Kreskin. He spoke about the "old days" in Reno, Nevada. The sincerity in his voice had no place to hide.

"I remember Bill Harrah and Pappy Smith. They built Reno." His eyes became a mirror of memories with streaks of joy and sadness. Leaning forward he asked, "Did you ever read Pappy Smith's book, *Always Leave Them Winners*? Pappy had a great philosophy about the casino business. A philosophy which I think the new corporate-run casinos should pay attention to. Pappy wanted enough people to leave as winners because they would always bring back others."

We got into a conversation about craps. I often wondered if someone could "think" a shooter into rolling a certain number. At a busy craps table you have a wide variety of bets all happening simultaneously. Pass line, don't pass, place bets, field bets, etc. Some players keep repeating a number over and over again silently in their minds. Others are more vocal and scream it out. The dice are receiving mixed signals. One player wants a six. Someone else is thinking ten. Then there's always someone biting their nails and screaming their lungs out for a hard eight. The dice are confused. The dealers are getting a headache.

But what would happen if all the players silently concentrated on *one* number? A meeting of the minds. Ten individual minds banding together for the same cause. A unison collaboration of mental energies focusing in on one number. Ten pass-line bettors thinking the "point." Could the dice receive and respond to this mental message?

Kreskin wasted little time in answering. "In the 1930s, a doctor at Duke University did a study on psychogenesis, better known as mind over matter. He researched parapsychology, by that I mean theopathy and other forms of clairvoyance, such as preceding information by some mental abilities.

"What caused him to do this study was the craps player. People were asked to think of certain numbers and the dice were rolled. Although he got very low statistical results in psychogenesis, he felt that the experiment was a success. His conclusion was that people can, by concentrating on certain numbers, control the throw of dice. But I've looked at the statistics and to me they don't seem to be significant.

"My ability is not in that area. I can perceive people's thought. In a craps game you're not working on what people have on their minds. You're working with an inanimate object, dice. I would have no advantage over the casino in a craps game. My advantage would be in any game dealing with cards where people are seeing information."

Like poker?

"There's no question in my mind that poker is the most skillful gambling game in the Western world. In poker, not only do you have to know your odds, you also have to know the physiology of your opponents. Blackjack at its most complicating level can't compare to the complexities involved in poker."

I was impressed with Kreskin's honesty and enthusiastic insight into the world of casino gambling. He told me about his private library with volumes and volumes of books on gambling. Kreskin has spent years studying statistics, analyzing every element, examining the rudiments and fundamentals of each game. "As a matter of fact," said Kreskin, "I have a record of every single blackjack game I've played."

We started debating the authenticity of systems. Do they work? Or do they make the player more susceptible to some flim-flam, air-mail special, $34.95 money-back guarantee, one-hour home study, winner's manual?

Kreskin reached for a glass of water. His thirst for sharing knowledge surpassed the dryness in his throat. His mind, like a computer bank, receives and stores data, files away anything that appears to be important, and deletes the nonessential surplus of trivial information. The ice-cubes weren't the only thing clicking when he placed his glass on the table. Somewhere in Kreskin's mind a page was found.

"You have to realize that casinos aren't built by winners. I think I'm familiar with almost all the systems. Some systems have proven that they do work. And when a system comes along that works, the casinos just change the rules. The new modified rules don't enable the system to work.

"I can't tell you how many pit bosses have told me this: 'Kreskin, if you want to have fun with a system go ahead. But the bottom line is this: When things are going your way at the tables, play. When things aren't going your way, don't play.' "

Simple logic for a complex emotion!

Casinos no longer bar Kreskin from playing. "I enjoy the exercise of playing. One rule I always follow is not to gamble in the hotel where I'm appearing."

Picking up a deck of cards, Kreskin said, "I have extraordinarily sensitive fingers." His long slender fingers began to shuffle the standard, 52-card deck. The cards fell indiscriminately one on top of the other. A fluttering, even rhythm bounced off the walls. His hands, like those of a casino dealer, moved effortlessly. No motion wasted, no strain. Wrist, hand, and fingers working together, like Itzhak Perlman playing a pawnshop violin and making it sound like a Stradivarius. Kreskin, with a $1.98 deck of Bee playing cards in his hands, was shuffling a masterpiece.

"I can memorize a shuffled deck of cards in 28 seconds, sometimes 22." Kreskin's voice rose above the shuffling sound. "I can cut instantly to any position in the deck."

Placing the shuffled deck on the table he said, "I want you to think of a card." There was a short pause. I could feel Kreskin's eyes looking at me. "Now tell me the card that you're thinking about."

I said, "The eight of diamonds."

"The eight of diamonds," repeated Kreskin.

I nodded, "Yes."

"Now, give me a number between 1 and 52."

I thought for a moment and said, "37."

Kreskin's answer was instantaneous. "You're off by one card. The eight of diamonds is the 38th card in the deck!"

Handing me the cards, he said, "Count them."

The 37th card was the four of clubs. Hiding beneath it was the eight of diamonds, the 38th card.

Did Kreskin read my mind? Was it autosuggestion? A card trick? Or could Kreskin be one of the world's greatest card mechanics?

"If I decided to go in the wrong direction in life," said Kreskin, "and become one of those ruthless people called card mechanics, I guess I would have a field day. But I haven't the slightest desire on the face of the earth to do that.

"I have a collection from the Sahara in Tahoe of cheating devices that have been taken away from people. Nobody has the faintest idea of the trouble people have gone through inventing these gadgets.

"My skill is in sensitivity. I used to sit with a deck of cards in my hands for seven hours a day. When I hold the deck I can feel 52 positions. I can pick up a deck of cards, and just by holding them in my hand, tell you how many cards are missing. If I riffle the deck twice, I can name the missing cards.

"People have asked me how I can memorize a deck of cards flashing by. You can't memorize a deck flashing by. What you have to do is see the cards in clumps, or clusters. You can cluster-memorize things. If you put 32 objects on this table I could — in 12 seconds — tell you every object. In spite of what anybody may say, you can't memorize a deck of cards by riffling through them. When I riffle though the deck something unconsciously figures that I only saw three 5's. Or that I only saw two aces.

"We don't realize the power of the mind. Most people rely on their sense of sight, hearing, and conversation. Our inner abilities are somewhat dulled!"

At the gambling tables, Kreskin plays conservatively. But on stage he's a high roller willing to lay his weekly fee on the line. A gutsy "one-shot" winner-take-all bet.

The rules are simple. First, you hire Kreskin, put an ad in the newspaper and watch the tickets disappear. Second, you hide Kreskin's fee for the night and cross your fingers. Using only his mental abilities, Kreskin must locate the check.

Do the odds favor Kreskin or the house? In 5,296 tries, Kreskin only heard "Seven out, line away," nine times!

I would like to thank Bill, Kreskin's road manager, for arranging this interview. And a special thanks to Kreskin for giving me two amazing hours!

Mister Mensa

Neon stars light the sky for all those neurotic zodiac players looking for that guiding magical light. Others hold hands and dial the casino hotline, 1-800-seance. A lucky jacket, a pinch of salt, right side, left side. Are casino players on a high-anxiety, self-induced run of kleptomania madness? Where have all the "intelligent" players gone?

"I'd rather not reveal my name," said the mystery caller, "but I got your number through a friend of a friend."

Right away I knew two things about the caller. First, he scored at or above the 98th percentile on a standard IQ test. Second, he's a casino player.

After a short pause I said, "Can I call you Mensa?"

Mensa is Latin for table. In 1945, Professor Cyril Burt thought it would be interesting to have a roundtable discussion with a panel of highly intelligent people. In 1990, I thought it would be interesting to have a phone conversation with a gambling Mensa member.

"I visit Atlantic City frequently," said the caller. "I enjoy playing craps because it gives me a chance to relax."

"But Mensa, I'm not interested in your relaxation. You belong to an organization that once had Albert Einstein as a member. You took an IQ test and scored higher than

98% of the general population. Someone with your intelligence just doesn't relax at the tables. You're different from the rest of us rail-squeezin', average-IQ craps players. Someone with your awareness and understanding of mathematical probabilities surely just can't rely on luck!''

"I'm sorry to disappoint you but I have no desire to sit down and actually explore the mathematical probabilities of dice. I'm just another pass-line bettor waiting for a hot shooter.

"To tell you the truth, you're better off not knowing the probabilities of dice. It spoils the fun. But this might be of interest to your readers. The probability of consistent winning rolls in craps by seven, eleven, or making the point is six in 25 for one win, and one in 582 for nine!''

"Yeah, right," I responded, like I could care less. Besides, his numbers were way off base, or I misunderstood him, or both.

"I love to play cards," said Mensa-caller number two. "Do you know the odds of getting a royal flush in poker? They're a little better than one in 649,739.* How about drawing all thirteen cards in the same suit? The odds of that happening are one in 158,753,389,899!

"Years ago, I loved playing blackjack and card-counting. At first it was exciting and challenging. But somewhere along the line it got boring. To me, a casino is a place where my mind gets a chance to take a catnap.

---

*Author's Note: With the typical video poker option of drawing up to five replacement cards, the odds of making a royal flush are about one in 40,000. Take that, Mensa!

"I love board games. Playing Scrabble for a few dollars is my kind of game."

O.K. We've covered Kreskin, Mensa, astrology, superstitions, and horoscope "science," looking for someone who might be able to beat the casino with their "extra powers." So far, nothing that would make a casino executive prop up his ears.

What we need is someone who can memorize a deck of cards forward and backward, or, at the very least, a few thousand digits of π.

Read on.

CHAPTER 13

Unforgettable

Memory: (a) a revival or reproduction of the memory image, (b) recognition of the image as belonging to the past of the remembering subject, and (c) temporal localization of the remembered object by reference to a psychological or physical time-scheme.

The Dictionary of Philosophy
by Ledger Wood.

Most of us have encountered a memory lapse at one time or another. You recognize a face but can't recall the person's name. We misplace keys or forget our zip code. Sometimes we have total recall of an event that happened 20 or 30 years ago, but can't remember what we had for dinner last night.

Our memory abilities are constantly tested and challenged when coming face to face with the technical and mathematical aspects of some casino games. Proficient, basic-strategy blackjack players rely on instant recall to determine the correct "play" on every hand.

Decisions on whether to hit, stand, split, or double-down, become a second reflex. Yet, that same basic-strategy player might find it impossible to remember their Social Security number.

Craps players caught up in the excitement of the game sometimes forget to take the odds behind their pass-line bets, or forget what numbers they've placed. At a roulette or baccarat table, players keep written score cards of previous numbers or winning hands.

There's a common fallacy among novice blackjack counters that overly exaggerates the mathematical process of counting. These people are under the misconception that card counters "memorize" every card dealt. Impossible? Inconceivable? For the average person, yes; but very feasible for a select few.

Dustin Hoffman's portrayal of an "idiot savant" in the movie Rain Man, opened our eyes to a wide-ranging disease called "autism." Hoffman won the Academy Award for his brilliant and sensitive performance of a man who had unbelievable memory capabilities, yet could not adapt to the outside world.

Medical journals define autism as an extreme self-preoccupation usually accompanied by withdrawal from reality. Absorbed in a fantasy life and being unable to relate to other people, the autistic person becomes pathological when that person loses contact with reality. He retreats into a private world of delusion and hallucination as a means of escape.

But as screenwriters Barry Morrow and Ronald Bass pointed out in the movie, an autistic person can have remarkable memory abilities, as evident in the scene where Hoffman recites a portion of the telephone book.

The scene most casino players remember took place at a blackjack table in Caesars Palace. Rain Man's ability to remember cards played from the shoe made the most astute card counters look like weekend players.

Originally, this chapter was going to be about an autistic person. Could someone like Rain Man really memorize a deck of cards? With the family's consent, and under the supervision of a doctor, I visited a hospital where I had the privilege to spend a few hours with an autistic person. But after witnessing the emotional impact on the family, I decided to discard the idea. Seeing a mother, on her weekly visit, kiss her child goodbye, makes the significance of this experiment shallow, indeed.

The subject of "memory" as it relates to casino games still held my interest, however. Could someone with an exceptional memory, plus a remarkable gift for math, turn the casino edge around to their side of the table?

Author and publisher, John Gollehon, sent me information about a man capable of storing 31,811 random numbers in his mind. This tip started a six-month investigation into a world of unexplainable memory capabilities. A world so phenomenal that someone can remember 50 digits faster than most of us can remember a phone number.

To give you an idea how the exceptional memory works, try this: Memorize the 30 numbers below in 30 seconds.

```
2 1 6 8 0 5 4 3 8 2
6 7 5 1 0 8 4 6 3 7
7 7 4 9 1 2 6 0 8 2
```

If you remembered 4 to 9 numbers, you're average. A recall of 10 to 19 numbers makes you extraordinary.

You might be considered brilliant if you remembered 20 to 29 numbers. If you remembered all 30 numbers, you're a genius.

Later in this chapter I'll introduce you to someone who can remember 50 digits, forward and backward!

From Manhattan, Kansas to Ithaca, New York, phone call after phone call brought me closer to finding someone with an extraordinarily gifted memory. I found myself researching a subject dating back hundreds of years. Unknown to me at the time, the person with the most exceptional memory in America was living 80 miles outside of Atlantic City. But first, a little history:

In the 1920s, S.V. Shereshevskii became the subject of a 30-year study under the supervision of Soviet psychologist A.R. Luria. Shereshevskii, a professional mnemonist (memory expert), previously studied music and worked as a journalist. He had total recall of everything he'd ever seen or heard. He could memorize tables of random digits and repeat their exact order fifteen years later! Being unable to forget anything — names, faces, conversations, and every shred of information — eventually led to emotional disorder. Those who studied him said he could not distinguish between a conversation he had five minutes ago from one he had five *years* ago! Sadly, Shereshevskii was committed to an asylum.

In another study, Psychologist I.M.L. Hunter interviewed and tested mathematics professor, A.C. Aitken. Hunter showed Aitken a list of 25 unrelated words. Twenty-seven years later, Aitken had total recall of all 25 words. Aitken showed a remarkable proficiency at remembering material that had a special meaning or interest to him. "His ability," concluded Hunter, "to discern properties and patterns of materials that interested him enabled him to organize information into complex conceptual maps.''

In a more recent test, E. Hunt and T. Love studied a Seattle man who could play seven games of chess simultaneously while blindfolded. He could also play 60 correspondence games without consulting written records. Referred to as V.P., this Seattle man could correctly recall a 48-digit matrix after only six minutes of study.

The Most Astonishing Memory

A five-year-old boy sits quietly in his room. With his face pressed against the window, he watches car after car park in front of his parents' house. A ''normal'' five-year-old might be attracted to the flashy colors or the sound of engines. Some may even daydream of sitting behind the wheel and driving through country roads or city traffic.

But this wasn't your run-of-the-mill five-year-old. Forty cars later, this astonishing five-year-old said, ''MYX1689.'' That was the first car to park in his parents' driveway. MYX554 was the second car; MYX558 was the third.

When the last guest left the party being hosted by his parents, their son recited — in the exact order in which they parked — the license plate numbers of all 40 cars!

Twenty-seven years later, and miles away from his Mangalore, India home, Rajan Mahadevan would become the subject of a $157,000 federal grant at Kansas State University.

''As a child,'' says Rajan, ''I used to be so lost in my own thoughts, I would talk to myself. It was hard to fit in. Other kids didn't know what to make of me."

Before attending graduate school where he studied biopsychology, Rajan previously studied engineering and business administration. "I was expected to make it big in life," said Rajan. "But my academic career was like the drawing of a mountain range!"

In an attempt to get his name in the Guinness Book of World Records, Rajan began studying computer print-outs of π.

For all of you readers who flunked basic geometry in high school, π is the theoretically infinite computation that measures the ratio of the circumference of a circle to its diameter, as expressed in the common equations: $C = \pi D$, where C is the circumference, and D is the diameter, and, $A = \pi R^2$, where A is the area of a circle, and R is the radius.

Pi, which begins at 3.14159, has no known duplication or pattern. From its starting point of 3.14159, π continues on indefinitely. Two mathematicians from Columbia University have calculated π to 480 million decimal places.

At the fifth International Congress on Yoga and Meditation held in Chicago, Rajan recited the first 10,000 numbers of π.

One year later in Mangalore, India, Rajan stood before a panel of judges for three hours and 49 minutes. He was reciting numbers so quickly that the judges had trouble keeping track.

Rajan's memory faltered when he "forgot" the 31,812th digit of π. The old record of 20,013 was shattered that day. On February 16, 1983, Rajan's name went into the Guinness Book of Records.

To most all of us, it would seem impossible that any-one could memorize over 31,000 numbers, in order. To really feel the impact of this incredible feat, we are presenting to you the first 5,000 digits of π.

To make the numbers "easier" to memorize, we have listed the numbers in lines of 10, and groups of 400. The numbers read left to right, across the page:

Pi Chart
3. +

1415926535	8979323846	2643383279	5028841971
6939937510	5820974944	5923078164	0628620899
8628034825	3421170679	8214808651	3282306647
0938446095	5058223172	5359408128	4811174502
8410270193	8521105559	6446229489	5493038196
4428810975	6659334461	2847564823	3786783165
2712019091	4564856692	3460348610	4543266482
1339360726	0249141273	7245870066	0631558817
4881520920	9628292540	9171536436	7892590360
0113305305	4882046652	1384146951	9415116094

3305727036	5759591953	0921861173	8193261179
3105118548	0744623799	6274956735	1885752724
8912279381	8301194912	9833673362	4406566430
8602139494	6395224737	1907021798	6094370277
0539217176	2931767523	8467481846	7669405132
0005681271	4526356082	7785771342	7577896091
7363717872	1468440901	2249534301	4654958537
1050792279	6892589235	4201995611	2129021960
8640344181	5981362977	4771309960	5187072113
4999999837	2978049951	0597317328	1609631859

5024459455	3469083026	4252230825	3344685035
2619311881	7101000313	7838752886	5875332083
8142061717	7669147303	5982534904	2875546873
1159562863	8823537875	9375195778	1857780532
1712268066	1300192787	6611195909	2164201989
3809525720	1065485863	2788659361	5338182796
8230301952	0353018529	6899577362	2599413891
2497217752	8347913151	5574857242	4541506959
5082953311	6861727855	8890750983	8175463746
4939319255	0604009277	0167113900	9848824012

8583616035	6370766010	4710181942	9555961989
4676783744	9448255379	7747268471	0404753464
6208046684	2590694912	9331367702	8989152104
7521620569	6602405803	8150193511	2533824300
3558764024	7496473263	9141992726	0426992279
6782354781	6360093417	2164121992	4586315030
2861829745	5570674983	8505494588	5869269956
9092721079	7509302955	3211653449	8720275596
0236480665	4991198818	3479775356	6369807426
5425278625	5181841757	4672890977	7727938000

8164706001	6145249192	1732172147	7235014144
1973568548	1613611573	5255213347	5741849468
4385233239	0739414333	4547762416	8625189835
6948556209	9219222184	2725502542	5688767179
0494601653	4668049886	2723279178	6085784383
8279679766	8145410095	3883786360	9506800642
2512520511	7392984896	0841284886	2694560424
1965285022	2106611863	0674427862	2039194945
0471237137	8696095636	4371917287	4677646575
7396241389	0865832645	9958133904	7802759009

9465764078	9512694683	9835259570	9825822620
5224894077	2671947826	8482601476	9909026401
3639443745	5305068203	4962524517	4939965143
1429809190	6592509372	2169646151	5709858387
4105978859	5977297549	8930161753	9284681382
6868386894	2774155991	8559252459	5395943104
9972524680	8459872736	4469584865	3836736222
6260991246	0805124388	4390451244	1365497627
8079771569	1435997700	1296160894	4169486855
5848406353	4220722258	2848864815	8456028506
0168427394	5226746767	8895252138	5225499546
6672782398	6456596116	3548862305	7745649803
5593634568	1743241125	1507606947	9451096596
0940252288	7971089314	5669136867	2287489405
6010150330	8617928680	9208747609	1782493858
9009714909	6759852613	6554978189	3129784821
6829989487	2265880485	7564012470	4775551323
7964145152	3746234364	5428584447	9526586782
1051141354	7357395231	1342716610	2135969536
2314429524	8493718711	0145765403	5902799344
0374200731	0578539062	1983874478	0847848968
3321445713	8687519435	0643021845	3191048481
0053706146	8067491927	8191197939	9520614196
6342875444	0643745123	7181921799	9839101591
9561814675	1426912397	4894090718	6494231961
5679452080	9514655022	5231603881	9301420937
6213785595	6638937787	0830390697	9207734672
2182562599	6615014215	0306803844	7734549202
6054146659	2520149744	2850732518	6660021324
3408819071	0486331734	6496514539	0579626856

1005508106	6587969981	6357473638	4052571459
1028970641	4011097120	6280439039	7595156771
5770042033	7869936007	2305587631	7635942187
3125147120	5329281918	2618612586	7321579198
4148488291	6447060957	5270695722	0917567116
7229109816	9091528017	3506712748	5832228718
3520935396	5725121083	5791513698	8209144421
0067510334	6711031412	6711136990	8658516398
3150197016	5151168517	1437657618	3515565088
4909989859	9823873455	2833163550	7647918535

8932261854	8963213293	3089857064	2046752590
7091548141	6549859461	6371802709	8199430992
4488957571	2828905923	2332609729	9712084433
5732654893	8239119325	9746366730	5836041428
1388303203	8249037589	8524374417	0291327656
1809377344	4030707469	2112019130	2033038019
7621101100	4492932151	6084244485	9637669838
9522868478	3123552658	2131449576	8572624334
4189303968	6426243410	7732269780	2807318915
4411010446	8232527162	0105265227	2111660396

6655730925	4711055785	3763466820	6531098965
2691862056	4769312570	5863566201	8558100729
3606598764	8611791045	3348850346	1136576867
5324944166	8039626579	7877185560	8455296541
2665408530	6143444318	5867697514	5661406800
7002378776	5913440171	2749470420	5622305389
9456131407	1127000407	8547332699	3908145466
4645880797	2708266830	6343285878	5698305235
8089330657	5740679545	7163775254	2021149557
6158140025	0126228594	1302164715	5097925923

0990796547	3761255176	5675135751	7829666454
7791745011	2996148903	0463994713	2962107340
4375189573	5961458901	9389713111	7904297828
5647503203	1986915140	2870808599	0480109412
1472213179	4764777262	2414254854	5403321571
8530614228	8137585043	0633217518	2979866223
7172159160	7716692547	4873898665	4949450114
6540628433	6639379003	9769265672	1463853067
3609657120	9180763832	7166416274	8888007869
2560290228	4721040317	2118608204	1900042296

6171196377	9213375751	1495951056	6049631862
9472654736	4252308177	0367515906	7350235072
8354056704	0386743513	6222247715	8915049530
9844489333	0963408780	7693259939	7805419341
4473774418	4263129860	8099888687	4132604721

"Just as you can't describe how you remember your phone number, neither can Rajan describe the process by which he remembers π," said memory expert Charles Thompson, a psychology professor at Kansas State University, who is conducting a study on Rajan's memory.

Now comes word of another memory expert who is not satisfied with remembering *only* 31,000 digits of π, but is going for an unheard of 100,000 (count 'em) digits. Surprisingly, this man is also from India. I wonder if it's something in the water?

But getting back to Rajan, Thompson still believes that Rajan may have the most remarkable numerical memory known to science, surpassing the 1920 study done on Shereshevskii.

"When it comes to remembering digits, Rajan is indeed exceptional," says Cornell Professor, Stephen J. Ceci. "And yet," continues Ceci, "his memory for other types of materials has been unremarkable," prompting examiners to conclude that:

> *"In our research with Rajan, we have observed dramatically different levels of proficiency, depending upon the nature of the material to be learned; that is, his memory performance appears to be content or material specific... In common parlance, Rajan's memory is at once extraordinary, average, and poor, depending on task and type of material."*   Charles Thompson

I asked professor Thompson if I could possibly talk to Rajan. Thompson told me that Rajan doesn't gamble, and therefore has no extensive knowledge of casino games. My opportunity to meet someone with superior memory proficiency seemed to hit a dead end.

"Just a minute," said Thompson. "Call professor Ceci at Cornell University. He might be able to help you."

Professor Ceci told me about "Bubbles P.," a 34-year-old man living 80 miles outside of Atlantic City. His memory capabilities have been the subject of an ongoing study at Cornell. Unlike Rajan, Bubbles P. does have an astute knowledge of casino games, plus an extraordinary insight into gamblers.

Three days later I received a 22-page report called, "Memory In Context: A Case Study Of 'Bubbles P.,' " written by Ceci, Michelle DeSimone, and Sarah Johnson. The report describes in detail various psychometric and information-processing tasks administered to Bubbles in an effort to better understand his mnemonic talent.

I called James Peronti, a.k.a. Bubbles, and expressed my interest in meeting him. James agreed to meet me at the Hamilton Mall, 12 miles outside of Atlantic City. Over six feet tall, and built like an NFL linebacker, James is a gentle and caring man. His concern and compassion for children overshadows his physique. James has appeared at many local schools demonstrating his remarkable memory abilities. "When kids see what I can do maybe they'll pay more attention to math," said James. "Maybe I could stop one kid from going the wrong way in life!"

I watched a videotape which showed James being tested at Cornell. Presented with a series of digits at a one-second rate, he was then asked to recall the digits backward. James was flawless, recalling 15 and 20 digits backward and forward.

In his report, Professor Ceci said, "James can recall digits forward and backward. It did not seem to matter to him in the slightest to be asked to recall the digits in one order, and then to recall them in reverse order. He volunteered to recall the digits in any order, including starting in the middle of the series and recalling first to the left, then to the right. Systematic testing confirmed he could do this at an errorless rate, up to a maximum of 20 digits."

I watched in amazement as James recalled any digit in the string, e.g., "give me the eleventh number from the left." An "average" person can recall seven digits forward, and only four digits backward. "By any standards," according to Ceci, "James is indeed statistically exceptional. His ability to recall forward and backward digits places him squarely in the top .001 percent of the population of adults!"

But how does he do it? "I really can't explain it," said James. "When I was a kid I thought everyone could do what I do!"

"We quickly ruled out any obvious tricks or recording strategies," said Ceci, "other than his self-reported attempt to segregate the stream of digits into 2's, 3's, or 4's when they were first presented to him (e.g., chunking the string 361839702428655910473 into the following triads: 361,839,702,428,655,910,473)."

The Warrington Face Recognition Test was given to James in order to assess other forms of memory. He was shown 50 black and white photographs and asked to remember them. After seeing the last photograph, subjects are presented 50 pairs of photographs, and instructed that one out of each pair of photos was already seen by them. James correctly recognized 45 out of 50, placing him around the 75 percentile for his age group.

Most people view each photograph at a 3 second rate. James preferred a much faster rate saying, "I'm good at reading faces because this is something that a poker player must do if he hopes to succeed. When I play poker, I play the player, not the cards!"

Professor Ceci showed James the following 50-digit matrix:

As another example:

6 6 8 0	4 2 3 7	2 7 6 8
5 4 3 2	3 8 9 1	1 9 2 6
1 6 8 4	1 0 0 2	2 9 6 7
7 9 3 5	3 4 5 1	5 5 2 0
		x 0 1 x

It took James 424 seconds, or a little over seven minutes, for him to memorize all 50 digits. Compared to other studies, his time was slightly longer. But he was able to recall it faster than any other mnemonist.

I couldn't believe what I was seeing as the camera got a close-up shot of the 50-digit matrix. Some of the numbers were blocked out. James was able to immediately identify specific numbers when cued by pointing to their corresponding empty cells in the blank matrix.

What's really remarkable is that six weeks later, James still had total recall of the entire 50-digit matrix!

"The rapidity with which he could recall digits in any location," says Ceci, "strongly suggests that James had a spatial code that enabled him to read out digits in any location. This interpretation is supported by his own self report; he claimed to see the matrix vividly."

James was asked to memorize a deck of cards. By accident, one card was missing from the deck. The cards appeared in the following order:

```
3  9  K  10 Q  7  A  5  Q  J  A  A  9  2  6  4  8  J
4  10 K  7  8  K  3  3  7  6  2  6  5  10 Q  2  8  4
4  9  Q  J  6  9  K  J  5  8  3  10 5  A  7
```

It would seem logical that if James could memorize a 50-digit matrix in seven minutes, he should be able to memorize 51 cards in seven minutes. His testers were surprised when five minutes later, James had total recall of all 51 cards.

It seems to me that one very important aspect of this test was overlooked by Ceci and his colleagues: James, a highly knowledgeable poker, gin, and pinochle player, could relate to a deck of cards more easily than random numbers.

"Immediately following our study of the playing cards," says Ceci, "James recalled the entire matrix backward and then forward without error. When asked to supply three specific cards that had corresponded to empty cells that he imagined (in other words, no empty matrix was supplied), he did so without error and usually within three seconds!"

Six weeks later, James returned to Cornell to continue his tests. Ceci thought it might be interesting to re-present a playing card matrix to James that he had not seen in six weeks. "This is the same matrix I saw last time," said James as he entered the room. Asked to explain how he knew that, James said, "the bottom row was the same as well as the top left corner of cards."

"In a post-experimental interview," wrote Ceci, "James insisted that he had not thought about the matrix in the intervening six weeks. He claimed that the bottom row 'jumped out at me,' signalling it was a matrix he had seen before. It was quite surprising to witness this behavior because it came at the end of approximately three hours of testing, during which he had seen many digits and playing cards."

You might be under the assumption that James is a Rhodes scholar with a doctorate in science or mathematics. This man, whose memory is so exceptional, has a high school diploma and a real-estate license. No Ivy League pennants, no alma mater, no college frat-house memorabilia.

Riding with me toward Atlantic City, James talked freely about his knowledge and attraction to gambling, and his physiological view into a gambler's mind. "A professional gambler has a very disciplined mind," said James as the Atlantic City skyline came into view. "Let's say that you have two people at a table. One is a tourist and the other makes his living gambling. Both players win $2,000. The tourist, who only gambles occasionally, will probably give back the $2,000 in one shot. The novice has no respect for a winning night.

"But the guy who gambles for a living places a higher value on the complexities of winning. He doesn't get carried away with the glitz-and-glamour emotions that romance the casino floor. The professional gambler has different priorities.

"Most people think that gambling is a simple cut-and-dry situation. You either win or lose. And to some extent that's true. But sometimes it's not what you win or lose. It's what you save!"

As we entered the casino, a noisy craps table caught our attention. Players were hunched over the table like hungry wolves eyeing a herd of sheep. The hot roll crescendoed into an outcry of verbal commands, "Press it, place the five, buy the 10, all the hardways." James and I were hearing the SOS before the fire goes out — a plea for help as the dice bounce their way into indiscriminate aftermath. But this time the players' pleadings went unanswered: "Seven out, line away" turned the body-heated wooden railing into an ice tray.

The wolves grumbled and growled as their parlay and press-bets fell victim to their greed. Accusations and fingers pointed everywhere. "The stupid shooter threw the dice like a jerk. Why did they change the stickman?"

Walking away from the table, James smiled and said, "People will always tell you who caused them to lose. But no one is ever gonna tell you that somebody else caused them to win. When people are losing they always find someone or something to blame. A shooter might throw the dice in an unorthodox manner and everyone blames him for their losses. But if that same shooter was making passes and numbers, his unorthodox style of throwing the dice would go unnoticed."

James doesn't just watch a craps game. His mathematical mind — which, I guess, never rests — had calculated every payout for the entire table, on every roll. One man doing the work of four! When I asked him how he does it, he just shrugged his shoulders and said, "I don't know!"

During dinner we exchanged casino stories. "I saw something at a craps table one night," said James, "that reinforces my convictions that some players have no common sense, or, acting out of greed, refuse to make a smart decision:

"A don't bettor was the only player at the table. He bet $8,000 on the don't side and on the come-out roll threw a six. He wanted a new point so he picked up his chips and walked away. To my way of thinking, he was in a 'no lose' situation. The biggest obstacle facing a don't bettor is throwing a natural on the come-out roll. He beat the natural. All he had to do now was place the six for $7,200. It's impossible for him to lose in this situation.

If he sevens out, he wins $800. If he makes the point, which was six, he wins $400.

"He could have done that all night with the other numbers. As long as he got past the naturals on the come out, he was home free. Either he was unaware of this fact, or he was greedy. A guy betting $8,000 a pop might not be satisfied winning four hundred, or eight hundred dollars. The gambling kick for him might not have been satisfied with one small win at a time. But the point is that at that moment he had the casino by the throat.

"Let's look at the same situation on a smaller scale. A $100 don't bettor gets past the natural and rolls a four. He buys the four, for $70, plus the $3 vig. If he sevens out he wins $27 ($100 minus $73). If he makes the four he wins $37 ($140 minus $103). But most players don't think that way.

"Here's something else about betting from the don't side. On the come-out roll, why is craps 12 a stand-off and not aces? The dice hit the wall and one die stops with a 6 showing and the other die is still spinning. The don't bettor knows three things instantly: (A) he can't win outright, (B) there's two ways that he can lose outright (6-1, 6-5), (C) he might get a stand-off if a point isn't established (6-6).

"But if the one die stopped with the number one showing, the player knows: (A) he can win outright two ways (1-1, 1-2), and (B) he can lose outright only one way (1-6)."

James Bubbles Peronti loves the atmosphere and energy that can only be found in a casino. He would like to utilize his memory abilities and in some capacity work in the casino industry. In my opinion, it would take a very creative personnel director to find the appropriate position for a man with his remarkable gift.

Professor Ceci wrote a letter of introduction for Peronti stating, "If you require the services of someone with tremendous potential for storing and recalling information, then Mr. Peronti is your man."

Driving back to the Hamilton Mall, where James had left his car, I asked him if he ever thought about being a card-counter. "A few days ago, I bought a book on blackjack," he responded. "If I can't get a job working on the casino's side of the tables, I might decide to work the *other* side of the tables!"

I wish to express my sincere gratitude to Professor Charles Thompson, from Kansas State University, Professor Stephen J. Ceci, and his colleagues, Michelle DeSimone and Sarah Johnson from Cornell University, for sending me their report, Memory In Context. And a special thank you to James Bubbles Peronti for driving over 80 miles just to visit with me. He is, perhaps, the only person who could beat the casino's blackjack tables with consistency. Yet, so far, he has not made any attempt to master the game.

Believe it, or not.

CHAPTER 14

America's
Biggest Casino

The biggest craps game in the world doesn't take place in Atlantic City — or Vegas. The world's biggest — and oldest — casino is in New York City, on Wall Street. Joe Granville, the guru of the stock market technicians, calls it "The Game." And where there's a "game" there are players. The Wall Street casino and the gambling casino have that one ingredient for success: the chance to make a quick buck.

Society has no problem accepting Wall Street. If you play the stock market, you're an "investor." If you play blackjack, you're a "gambler." If you play both, you're simply an "investor" who likes to "gamble." A psychiatrist might say you're a "masochist."

The two worlds are similar and dissimilar in many ways. The names for the Wall Street casinos would somehow seem out of place flashing on a neon sign. Imagine walking down the Boardwalk and seeing these names in flashing lights: Paine Webber, Merrill Lynch, Prudential-Bache, Smith Barney — boring! And besides, who wants to make money the old-fashioned way?

Imagine telling your friends, "I won $2,500 last night shooting craps at Shearson Lehman Brothers." A rose by any other name is still a rose. Maybe that works in the world of poetry, but not in the casino world. Caesars, Taj Mahal, Harrah's, Sands — names that have drawing power for those who wish to "invest" at the tables.

Wall Street uses blue chips. Casinos use a variety of colored chips: white, red, green, black, and that IBM of the casino floor — orange.

You buy into a stock; you buy into a game. In a casino, it's you against the house. On Wall Street, it's you against the house.

Casino dealers are visible; stockbrokers exist only on the phone. Investors study a stock for months before buying. A craps shooter watches a table for two seconds before buying in.

Yelling and screaming are acceptable on both floors.

Friends recommend stocks that are hot. Friends recommend dealers that are cold.

Every day at 4 o'clock a bell rings on Wall Street. Every day at 4 o'clock someone is hoping that a bell will ring in Atlantic City.

If you lose $1,000 in the stock market, your spouse will understand. Lose $1,000 in a casino and your spouse will kill you!

One has "money market funds," the other has "money market *fun*." Casinos have the "drop" and Wall Street has the Dow Jones average.

One hundred dollars on Wall Street is a joke. Fifty dollars in Atlantic City, and you're in business.

The terminology used in the two casino worlds is related:

Wall Street:	"commission" is the amount paid to a broker to buy or sell.
Atlantic City:	commission at a baccarat table is paid to the casino only when you win.
Wall Street:	a "bull" is one who believes the market is heading upward.
Atlantic City:	a bull is one who sits in the coffee shop at 4 a.m. telling you he just won $10,000 and then asks you to pay for his eggs because he left his wallet in his room.
Wall Street:	"hedging" is trying to minimize your risk by taking certain steps to offset the risk.
Atlantic City:	hedging is playing two slot machines at once.
Wall Street:	"liquidation" is the process of converting securities or other property into cash.
Atlantic City:	liquidation is a J&B on the rocks.
Wall Street:	"naked option" is an option written against stock which is not currently owned.
Atlantic City:	naked option is a showgirl's nightmare.
Wall Street:	"random walk" is a theory that cannot predict a stock's action or direction as a result of its previous moves.
Atlantic City:	random walk is looking for a dealer who breaks.
Wall Street:	"stop order" specifies a particular price at which a stock should be bought or sold.

Atlantic City: stop order is your wife telling you it's time to go home.

Wall Street: "tax shelter" is any means whereby income receives preferential tax treatment.

Atlantic City: tax shelter is never cashing out over $10,000.

Wall Street: "selling against the box" is short selling against stock which is owned by an investor.

Atlantic City: selling against the box is never making any "prop" bets at the craps table.

Wall Street: "stock split" is the allotment of additional shares to stockholders.

Atlantic City: stock split is someone splitting "tens."

Wall Street: "private placement" is selling securities directly to one or more large investors.

Atlantic City: private placement is a room "comp."

Wall Street: "odd lot" is a trade of fewer than 100 shares.

Atlantic City: odd lot is what the dealers see every day.

Wall Street: "limited partnership" is a form of investment often employed because of favorable tax consequences.

Atlantic City: limited partnership is when you're winning and your friend isn't.

Wall Street: "dividend" is a payment distributed to shareholders.

Atlantic City: dividend is a blackjack table that offers the player "surrender."

Wall Street: "coupon bond" is a bond with interest coupons attached.

Atlantic City: coupon bonds are passed out to the bus people before they can go to the restrooms.

Wall Street: "clearing house" is a corporation which takes the opposite side of all trades.

Atlantic City: clearing house is a dealer drawing a seven-card 21!

Wall Street: "annual report" is a financial statement issued to shareholders.

Atlantic City: annual report is your husband walking over to your slot machine every 15 minutes and looking in your coin bucket.

Wall Street: "support level" is a term which denotes a price area.

Atlantic City: support level is a "don't" bettor telling a "pass line" bettor that he's losing his shirt.

Wall Street: "uptick" is a transaction made at a price higher than the preceding transaction.

Atlantic City: uptick is the roulette ball bouncing into your number.

Wall Street: "technical analysis" is the study of patterns and price movement, in an attempt to forecast the future of the market or individual stocks.

Atlantic City: technical analysis is someone who wears a rabbit's foot around their neck.

Atlantic City and Wall Street, so much alike and yet different. People come to Atlantic City for fun and excitement. Sinatra doesn't sing on Wall Street. Rodney Dangerfield might get "no respect" on Wall Street, but he sure gets a lot of laughs here.

A blackjack player from Brooklyn, New York had this to say: "My father plays the market. He buys a stock and then he can't sleep at night. Is it gonna go up or down? Did I do the right thing? Me, I play blackjack. Win or lose, I sleep like a baby. Who needs the stress? Besides, my father's the kinda guy who would stand on a soft 15!"

The casino industry always seems to be under the magnifying glass of suspicion. Skeptics are constantly looking for scandal, someone or something that could be used to discredit the casino industry. If you're looking for headlines about greed and corruption, turn to the financial page.

Unscrupulous activities over the last few years have shown us that greed is an addiction; inside trading; banks laundering drug money; stock fraud; the savings and loan scandal; Michael Milken, the "junk bond whiz," indicted on 98 counts; Drexel Burnham Lambert, polluting the stock exchange floor like an Exxon tanker, and dishing out $350 million in executive bonuses before heading to bankruptcy court.

The oldest casino in the world fell victim to man's oldest sin: hypocrisy.

CHAPTER 15

A Day In The Life

Have you ever wondered what a typical day in the life of a casino president is like? Do they sit around all day in some lavishly decorated office suite reading old Mickey Spillane novels and call their secretaries "doll"? Does their day start at 2 p.m., and end when the last shooter sevens out?

In a Hollywood movie from the 60s, you *might* see a casino president wearing a silk monogrammed robe — a glass of champagne in one hand, a stack of thousand-dollar bills in the other — sitting behind a desk the size of a football field and watching over his domain on private, wall-to-wall television monitors.

But this is Atlantic City, not Hollywood.

Most of us are only familiar with the action on the casino floor. But high above the casino there's a hotel president making million-dollar decisions every day. The job is glamorous, prestigious, and financially rewarding for those who can survive the pressures. Nerves of steel, diplomacy, and a dash of savoir-faire are required for this 24-hour-a-day job.

Said a retired casino executive, "In this business, you can smell like a rose on Monday, and be a thorn in the corporation's ass on Tuesday!"

I had the opportunity to spend the day with one of Atlantic City's most outstanding and respected hotel presidents. His creative and enthusiastic approach to the casino industry, plus his devotion to the community and numerous charities, set him apart from the others.

My intention was to shadow a hotel president and write about his daily activities. But the man who I chose to shadow had so many interesting things to say that it turned into one of the most enlightening interviews during my 15 months of research.

As I entered the elevator I checked my watch. I was right on time. Five floors later I was shaking hands with Roger P. Wagner, president and chief operating officer of the Claridge Hotel and Casino.* I made it to the fifth floor by pushing a button. Wagner's journey up the corporate ladder wasn't that easy. His elevator made a few unexpected stops along the way.

Wagner's childhood dream was to become an architect. His idols were probably Frank Lloyd Wright or Philip Johnson. But his dream turned into a "calculus" nightmare his first semester at the University of Idaho. "I struggled with calculus," said Wagner. "It just was not my bag."

So what does an 18-year-old, disillusioned architect do when life deals him his first setback? If you're Roger

---

*Shortly before this book went to press, Wagner became president of Trump Castle.

Wagner, you put on your running shoes and run. And you keep on running until the University of Nevada in Las Vegas gives you a track scholarship.

"I wasn't sure what I wanted to do my first year at UNLV. For one semester I majored in education. Later, I switched to Hotel Administration."

Wagner's marathon run from Idaho to Nevada was only a warm-up. It would take Wagner 19 years and over 3,000 miles to jog his way to the presidency of the Claridge. He might have traded in his sneakers for a pair of leather shoes, but he's still running. Only this time nobody's chasing him!

Wanted: Front-desk clerk, Dunes Hotel!

That sign posted on the wall in the college's executive office would be the turning point in Wagner's life.

"I didn't even know what the hell a desk clerk was! The only time I'd been in a casino was to run in, take a dip in the swimming pool, and run out. It was the thing that kids did in those days when we were out cruising the strip.

"I applied for the job and was hired. That summer, I went to school during the day and worked nights. Along came Labor Day, and in those days Vegas buttoned itself up in the fall just like this town used to. The hotel started to lay people off. But a job opened up on the graveyard shift and I took it. I worked the graveyard for three years."

There really is no such thing as a "typical day" for Wagner. Most mornings he's at his desk by 8 a.m. His workday ends 12 or 14 hours later... six days, sometimes seven days a week. "I'm a workaholic. My friends constantly kid me about my supposed boundless energy. Fortunately, I don't require too much sleep."

Wagner's work ethic didn't start the day he became president of the Claridge. Let's backtrack to Vegas, 1969.

Twenty-two years old and fresh out of college, Wagner, with a B.S. in Hotel Administration, and a Masters in enthusiasm, went job hunting. The Sands Hotel offered Wagner a bet he couldn't refuse: a 90-day, test-period job as a desk clerk. If Wagner proved himself, the Sands would promote him to assistant hotel manager. It was a no-lose situation for the house and the player. Ninety days later the Sands had a new assistant hotel manager. Wagner's hot roll was just beginning.

In 1973, when Howard Hughes owned everything in Vegas — including the Sands — Wagner, sensing no promotional opportunities, resigned. He was beginning to learn how to play "musical chairs" casino-style.

Wagner went back to where he started — the Dunes. Only this time he wasn't a desk clerk. His new position was hotel manager. Eleven months later, the music stopped. But this time Wagner found a more lucrative chair. The Frontier Hotel — owned by, you guessed it, Howard Hughes — became Wagner's home for the next two years.

The Hughes organization, sensing the potential and ambition in Wagner, transferred him back to the Sands. His new position: assistant general manager.

"In 1977, my ex-boss from the Frontier, who was now president of the MGM in Reno, offered me a job as executive vice president."

So, with twelve years of casino experience under his belt, and having just turned 29, Wagner left Vegas.

"I watched the building of that hotel from the ground up. We opened in 1978. It's a common occurrence in our business that the first (management) team often gets fired. Well, it did. I was washed down with the team. It was a very excruciating experience."

Wagner's eyes drifted to the window. The scars of that "excruciating experience" were still evident as Wagner searched for solace in the blue and white November sky. His eyes looked cheerless, but only for a moment. Smiling, he said, "I think everyone in this business should be fired once!" Turning to me he added, "I really believe that."

Out of work, Wagner returned to the Sands Hotel in Las Vegas for the third time. Dick Danner, president of the Sands, offered Wagner a job in the purchasing department. Eighteen months later, Wagner was promoted to executive vice president of the Sands. In 1981, the Pratts purchased the Sands. Six months later, Wagner was playing musical chairs again. Resigning from the Sands, Wagner moved on to become vice president and general manager of the Edgewater Hotel and Casino in Laughlin.

"The Edgewater was a highly-leveraged new casino that opened without enough money. We had a lot of licensing difficulties. I was brought in by one of the owners that remained who didn't lose his license during the opening. We undertook a sale. I said I would try to keep it from going into bankruptcy. About 15 months later we sold it to Circus Circus."

I always thought it was the player on the casino floor who faced the unforeseeable... the illogical whims of fate. But if getting to the top of the casino hierarchy is the same dealing of hot and cold cards, then Wagner has, like so few of us, truly mastered the game.

In 1983, Bill Dougall, President of the Claridge, put the word out that he was looking for a vice president of hotel operations. The general manager of the Barbary Coast in Vegas called Dougall and recommended Wagner. The rest, as they say, is history. When Dougall resigned, Del Webb appointed Wagner president and chief operating officer of the Claridge. The long-distance runner of the casino world finally got a chance to catch his breath. Or did he?

"The nature of our business requires us to conduct reasonable office hours during the week. But it's not all office work. I set time aside every day and frequently walk through the casino and the other sections of the hotel. Of course, weekends are our busiest so I generally work later on Saturdays.

"I try to take Sundays off but that's not always possible. This coming Sunday is the closing night of our production show, George M. Traditionally, I go on stage and toast the cast.

"There are enough senior-level people in the bureaucracy of Atlantic City casinos to be around the place seven days a week, 24 hours a day."

Here's an example of Wagner's weekday calendar:

8 a.m.

Wagner, who serves as president of the United Way in Atlantic County, meets with United Way director, Ray Jacoby.

9 a.m.

Board meeting. The board will address the topic of incentives for the new year.

10 a.m.

Wagner meets with interior designer Charles Silverman. The Claridge is embarking on some major internal renovations. Wagner's knowledge of architecture will play a big part in his final decision. A follow-up meeting is scheduled with Silverman and the hotel's executives to discuss the designer's proposal.

11 a.m.

Review cost-cutting ideas with VPs.

12 noon

Company officers meet with Wagner to arrange a three day strategic planning conference.

1 p.m.

Wagner has a staff meeting with the casino's pit bosses.

2 p.m.

Wagner attends the taping of a television show, which is set at the Claridge.

3 p.m.

All directors are summoned to attend a two-hour meeting in Wagner's office.

5 p.m.

Wagner makes a guest appearance on Tom Regan's radio show.

On an average day, Wagner receives 80 to 100 phone calls. And according to his secretary, he finds time to answer or return every one.

The day Wagner and I met, he had just returned from a one-hour meeting with Ron Lenczycki, executive vice president of Harrah's. Great, I thought to myself, this is the way I envisioned this business. Two high-level casino guys rolling up their sleeves and talking about the "blood and guts" battles on the casino floor. I was only half right. They did talk about blood. Wagner and Lenczycki are co-chairmen for the South Jersey Red Cross blood drive.

A very important part of Wagner's day is spent walking through every department in the hotel. Wagner suggested that I tag along with him. Our first stop was the hotel's lobby.

"Sometimes the best ideas come from our employees," said Wagner. Pointing to an empty booth he said, "That used to be our customer service area. An employee suggested that we move it across the lobby. Not only did it enhance the lobby's appearance, but it also got rave reviews from our customers."

I tried to stay a few steps behind Wagner as we entered the casino. Wagner's energetic pace made it easy. My entire focus was on the employees' reaction to seeing their president. Would they freeze, or suddenly stand at attention? Would they act nervous?

Wagner stopped and said hello to a security guard. A cleaning lady, recognizing her boss, smiled hello. "Nice to see you," said Wagner. "How are you?"

Passing the table games, Wagner acknowledged a few players. Dealers, pit bosses, and floor persons looked confident and relaxed. The games were running smoothly. "Hello Mr. Wagner," echoed as we passed table after table. The Claridge employs approximately 2,500 people. It wouldn't surprise me if Wagner knew most of them by name.

The Claridge is the only casino in Atlantic City that has gambling on three floors. The entire third floor is devoted to the slot player. "We designed this floor with the bus patron in mind," said Wagner. One look and you can understand what Wagner meant. The third floor is certainly a slot player's haven: a wide variety of machines and easy access to the restaurants.

By Atlantic City standards the Claridge is a small casino. But don't let the size fool you.

April 1990, Donald Trump's Taj Mahal says "open sesame." The existing ten casinos watch in amazement as the Taj takes in a record $34.4 million for the month of April. Like a neighborhood bully, the Taj muscled in on everyone's bottom line. And while the world's largest casino was flexing its 120,000-square-foot casino-floor muscles, Atlantic City's smallest casino, the Claridge, refused to be bullied around.

Despite its size, the Claridge was one of only two casinos to show a year-to-year increase in revenue for the month of April when the Taj opened. While the big guys were nursing their revenue wounds, the Claridge, after years of struggling and being labeled "the underdog," became an overnight contender. Atlantic City's smallest casino didn't have a knockout punch. But it sure knocked the wind out of all those ringside doubters.

Wagner theorized on the management and marketing strategy for the Claridge. "We try to do a team concept and set our basic strategic objectives in place. We've taken the position that we can't be what the big guys are. We don't have the resources and we don't have the physical property. On the other hand we have something they don't have. And that's the smallness and the closeness of staff. Our main goal is to truly provide greater and friendlier customer service than anyone else in town."

Every casino claims to be "friendlier." But are they? And exactly what should we, the customer, expect from a casino staff. Why should you or I go to casino A when casino B has the same games? For a moment, let's forget about the astute player who looks for single-deck blackjack games or triple-odds craps tables.

Does Mr. & Mrs. Average Player really care about odds and playing conditions? Or is their main concern a friendly casino atmosphere? Two days after my visit with Wagner I decide to find out.

It was a typical Saturday night as I weaved my way through the crowded casino floor at the Claridge. There's nothing like a busy Saturday night to test a dealer's patience and a player's tolerance. I talked to players and dealers. Here is a sample of their opinions on the subject:

"It's hard to smile all the time," said a blackjack dealer. "I always try to be polite to everyone who sits at my table. There's more to this job than just shuffling and dealing cards eight hours a night. The longer you're in this business the more you realize that customers expect a smiling, friendly dealer. I think most of the dealers in Atlantic City would agree with me. We've all matured over the years. Two months ago I went to Vegas for the first time. Dealers there seem to hustle the players for tokes."

"The younger, inexperienced dealers have to realize that people come here to escape the everyday hassles," said a craps dealer. "The last thing they need is to be hassled by a dealer or a floor person. When I worked in Vegas, I remember an entire dice crew being fired for hustling tokes. There's a "hustle" attitude in Nevada that doesn't exist here. Believe me, I should know. I worked out there for 25 years before coming to Atlantic City."

The players I talked to were all in agreement on one thing: The main reason they continue to patronize the same casino is exactly what Wagner has been stressing to his staff — a friendlier environment. It's a loser's pacifier and a winner's playpen!

The Claridge has a campaign slogan that reads, "Claridge... because we're smaller and friendlier."

Wagner's employees seem to be living up to that slogan.

"Your employees have to believe that they are the best," said Wagner. "We're not going to be number one in revenue, or bottom line. But we can be number one in friendliness. We want to get everybody customer oriented.

I asked Wagner if he ever feels the pressure from the casino floor if someone is winning large sums of money. What would he do if a player like Akio Kashiwagi, a.k.a. the Warrior, came in and bet $200,000 a hand?

"The gambling aspect of our business doesn't make me nervous," said Wagner. "You have to set your gambling limits based on what your company can afford to lose. I would not book bets of that size at the Claridge. I don't have the bankroll to pay him if he beats me. And I don't have any other customers of his stature to offset a big win.

"When I worked at the Sands in Vegas we used to cater to some of the world's highest rollers. But the Sands was bankrolled to cater to that type of customer.

"We're really in a business that rents space and time, in all our games, whether it be slots or table. In return, we don't give the customer true odds. We give them slightly less than true odds, which is called the house advantage. That's how we collect the rent. That's the admission ticket to our Disneyland. The only difference is that some customers pay full admission and others get in for free!''

Although the Claridge has its share of the high-roller market, it seems to cater more to the average player.

''We cater to the kind of customer,'' said Wagner, ''that's not going to beat us out of a lot of money. And we're not going to beat *them* out of a lot of money. Our biggest payouts have been through slot machine jackpots. Someone hit a $925,000 jackpot on one of our progressive machines. I think it still remains the biggest jackpot ever paid on a quarter machine. There's $2 million in jackpots down there right now. If someone hits, God bless them. I'm prepared to pay.

''Sometimes we get whacked around on our table games. A customer won $500,000 at a craps table one night. On the other hand, we've never beaten anyone out of $500,000 either. We can win and we can lose. But in the long run, 10,000 hands with the same customer, we're going to be on the plus side!''

As Wagner talked, it became evident to me that he did more than just work in Vegas. He observed the sights and sounds that run through a casino. The casino floor is, after all, the bloodline that keeps the heart and soul of a casino/hotel on life support. I can only assume that Wagner has seen one too many transfusions turn into a malpractice nightmare.

''This is a very cyclical business. You have to have a stomach for gambling. The old timers understood this business. They grew up in the business. Maybe they were bookies, or ran illegal backroom games. But in Vegas, they ran legitimate gambling houses. They knew that their bread and butter was the customer. They weren't afraid to lose because they knew that, in the long run, the customer will come back if he has your money.

"Too many people in the business today don't understand that. If a player wins they say, 'They've got our money.'

"No, they don't. They have *their* money. They won it."

I told Wagner about an experience I had one night at Resorts. It was a Saturday night and I had just finished working a high-roller party. The casino was crowded but it lacked an air of excitement. Suddenly, heads began turning and you could feel that something was happening. Walking through the casino was Merv Griffin. Customers, young and old, were shaking his hand as if he were an old friend. Merv's personality lit up the casino. I asked Wagner if he thought this was a move back to the old Vegas days when owners would walk the casino floor.

"A lot of the old-timers came out of the entertainment business. Jack Entratter worked at the Copa in New York before he became president of the Sands. He started the high-end entertainment policy by booking Sinatra.

"A true entrepreneur like Donald Trump, Steve Wynn, or Merv Griffin can use their celebrity status as a marketing tool. Merv's getting more and more involved in the business. He walks through the casino, the kitchens, the offices. Employees want to be recognized. They want to be a part of a successful team.

"I try to remind the executives here at the Claridge to always remember where they came from. This floor (executive offices) intimidates employees. Sometimes we forget how intimidated we used to be by the officers of the company. When I was younger, and working at the Dunes, I remember being called up to the president's office. First of all, I didn't know how to get to the president's office. I was nervous as hell thinking that I was going to be fired. It turned out that a customer had written a letter to the hotel president praising me for doing a fine job.

"That experience taught me a very important lesson. You don't call people to your office. You go down to their area. It's very intimidating for an employee to have to come up to the boss's office!"

Talking about Donald Trump, Wagner said, "Trump is very demanding but he's also very good to his employees. He wants things to happen quicker than they can in this kind of business. He has some very competent people working for him. But in this business you can't be quick. It took me several years to turn the Claridge around."

The current state law prohibits casino employees involved in gambling activities from gambling in the casinos. Personally, I feel that the law is ludicrous. Wagner concurred:

"I would like to see the law changed in New Jersey that would allow casino employees to gamble. Maybe, if they sat on the other side of the table, they might see the kind of crap that customers have to take sometimes from casino employees. I go to Vegas three or four times a year to visit grandchildren. My mother and father, God bless them, live in Boulder City, Nevada. Although I'm not an avid gambler, I like to sit down and play black-jack, or shoot craps. It gives me the opportunity to see how different and relaxed it is in other markets. At some point I think the laws will change here.

"I'm not a proponent of trying to beat your employees out of their paychecks. I think that's wrong. In some places in Nevada, that does occur. Down in Laughlin, case in point, we used to run a third of our payroll back (to the casino). But that is not in the best interests of your employees.

"Pappy Smith (founder of Harold's Club in Reno) once said, 'I gotta win my money six times before it's mine. The customer is gonna steal from me. Employees are gonna steal from me. So if I keep grinding it through six times, it finally belongs to me.' "

As the day wore on, Wagner's energy never showed signs of slowing down. He's a relaxed and confident man. Wagner can project authority in a non-domineering way. I doubt if there's an egotistical bone in his body.

The so-called glitz and glamour of the casino business has blinded many men. Blurred integrity is the casino's answer to the businessman's ulcer. Wagner's 20/20 vision refuses to weaken. The employees at the Claridge don't fear Wagner; they respect him. In return, Wagner offers them his trust.

"This is a business where you don't have a lot of trust, industry-wise," said Wagner. "The state sets the rules. You've got B watching A, C watching B, D watching C. Who the hell watches Z? At some point, you have to have trust. Fortunately for me, I have a staff of people that I trust."

Atlantic City casinos have fallen victim to the stringent rules set forth by the Casino Control Act. Most casino executives feel that New Jersey is over-regulated. The Division of Gaming Enforcement and the Casino Control Commission are the two regulatory agencies that enforce the Casino Control Act.

The cost to regulate the casino industry in Nevada is around $16 million. In New Jersey, it's a staggering $59 million annually. Nevada has 285 casinos, New Jersey has twelve! Who picks up the tap for the baker's dozen? The casinos, who else. Can you think of another industry where you pay inflated prices for inflated regulations?

The subject of regulations in New Jersey can no longer be avoided. Casinos in New Jersey are drowning in regulations while Nevada casinos swim in the luxury of a less regulated, and less costly environment.

Wagner's eyes pointed to a book on his desk. "You see that book in front of you? That's a book with all the casino regulations."

As I eyed the thickness of the book I remembered something someone once told me. "The Casino Control Commission's book on regulations is like a hemorrhoid that won't go away. And every casino in town is constipated!"

Steven Perskie, chairman of the CCC, has requested that a committee be formed to evaluate — chapter by chapter — the book on casino regulations. Wagner, along with the other CEO's, are on that committee.

"We are going to make proposals to the CCC and the legislators," said Wagner, "of changes we believe need to be made that are in the best interests of the industry, the state, and the public — (changes that) will not hurt the integrity of the business. We're all in agreement that the integrity issues on the table and identified in that book are important.''

Everyone is always questioning the integrity of the casino industry. I haven't seen any casino executives going to jail recently, but Keating and his S&L pals are doing some time. A junk-bond whiz might even be their cellmate.

Yet, the casino industry is constantly under the magnifying glass of suspicion as evident in Wagner's next comment:

''Why should we be required to spend nine dollars to make sure one dollar doesn't get stolen? That's what is ludicrous about some of these regulations and the way they are written. Maybe they were appropriate in 1978 when the casino industry opened, but now they need to be modified.''

I asked Wagner how the regulations affect his decisions on the casino floor. Does he need the commission's approval to move a slot machine, or introduce four-deck blackjack? Is there a tremendous amount of "red tape" involved? Do the regulations hinder casino operations?

''In the case of four-deck blackjack,'' said Wagner, ''that's an internal control situation which in 90 days we were able to have approved. We can go from eight, six, four, or two decks by notifying the commission one day in advance. If we wanted to move a slot machine we have to notify the commission one day in advance.''

Do these regulations seem fair and reasonable? Or are they the handcuffs of a bureaucracy where no one can find the keys? Here's an example of what I mean:

Let's say that we own a casino. It's 1 a.m. and a player wants to play blackjack — $1,000 a hand — at a single-deck game. What do we tell the guy? "Gee, sir, if you have nothing better to do could you just hang around for 24 hours while we call the CCC?"

Shouldn't the casino have the right to honor or deny the player's request? Wasn't America built on free enterprise?

Wagner went on to explain another regulation that he feels needs to be changed:

"Let's say that tomorrow I'm going to bring in a Venezuelan group that likes to play roulette. To make them more comfortable, I decide to pull out six blackjack tables and replace them with four roulette tables. Right now, I can't do that. I can't move a whole base of table games without a complete 90-day submission. And then I have to get an architect and lawyers involved. We should have more flexibility."

As chairman of the committee looking into casino regulations, Wagner is devoting all his attention to chapter 47, better known as Rules of the Games. "This is a very controversial issue," said Wagner. "The rules need to be changed. My personal opinion is to let free enterprise handle it like it does in Nevada."

Some casinos weren't too thrilled by that statement.

"I won't mention any names," said Wagner, "but some casinos like regulations. They really don't want to compete in table games and I think they're wrong. Instead, they want to compete in other areas like big-name entertainers or giant suites. Competing in table games might not fit in with their basic financial structure right now."

The excitement generated by casinos competing in table games would benefit the Atlantic City player *and* the casinos. Vegas was built on competition. It might be time for Atlantic City to rekindle that stimulating atmosphere created by Las Vegas casino owners. Sometimes, progress takes a giant step backward!

"We're trying to write rules," said Wagner, "that will give flexibility, if nothing else to expediting a test. For instance, with surrender*, we had to write a very extensive (presentation to the CCC) as to the effects on this rule change on the public and on our bottom line. Well, how the hell do we know until we test it? We can say we think this will happen, or we believe that this will happen.

"Currently under the law the test is for 90 days. But cycles in this business are such that 90 days is not enough time to do a test."

Not only do I agree with Wagner's position on the 90-day test period, but I've seen how it can affect the public.

Resorts recently introduced five-times odds at their craps tables. They, like the Claridge, ran a 90-day test period. At the end of the test period Resorts asked for an extension. They needed more time to evaluate the new ruling. The state said "no," and Resorts had to discon-

---

*Surrender is a player option at blackjack whereby the player, after seeing his initial two cards, can throw in his hand and "surrender" only one-half of his original wager. For example, a player will typically surrender his hand on counts of 15 and 16 (but not 8–8) if the dealer has a 10-value card showing. The player option on this rule (highly favorable to the player) is more involved than our simple example, especially if the player is counting the cards.

tinue its odds. They reapplied to do another test which started 30 days later.

In the meantime, players got confused. "What do you mean no more five-times odds? Don't give me some crap about a 90-day test. What the hell are you guys trying to pull here? You won't see me in this joint anymore!"

Wagner summed up the solution: "We believe a test should be continued, and then the success of the test should be determined by the property, not the state. I'm going to be proposing that a test could be continued without interruption. We shouldn't have to quit the test during the analysis and the approval process."

To attract new customers, a retail store displays the word "sale" in its window. When casinos offer players advantageous rules, that's their neon "sale" sign. By reinstating surrender to blackjack, the Claridge attracted a new group of bargain hunters.

"Let the free market dictate what we should offer," said Wagner. "Right now we're so competitive that nobody is going to do stupid rules."

I asked Wagner why he thinks the other casinos haven't followed his lead. Why is the Claridge the only casino with surrender blackjack?

"The rest of the industry doesn't understand surrender. They don't know the effects of it and they're not willing to put it on their tables. The law states that if you want surrender you must put it on all your tables or none at all. But if the law said you can put surrender on any selective tables you want, then I bet this entire town would have surrender tables."

I asked Wagner how the surrender ruling affected the casino's drop percentage*. To calculate the drop percentage, you divide the win by the drop*. If the drop box at a blackjack table has a total of $20,000 in cash and markers and is winning $2,000, the drop percentage for that game is 10%, ($2,000 divided by $20,000).

"Originally, we didn't want it on our four-deck games. We only wanted it on our eight-deck tables. So we ran a controlled test in two identical pits. One pit dealt four decks, the other eight. They both had the same drop. The only difference was that the eight-deck tables held 1½% (drop percentage) more than the four-deck tables. Surrender is an option that a lot of our customers like. The nice thing about surrender is that it's their option. If they want to use it, fine. If they don't want to use it, that's fine, too."

I was writing a monthly gaming column when the Claridge reinstated four-deck blackjack with surrender. I conducted a survey in which I asked $25-per-hand players and up why they were playing eight-deck shoes

---

*The "drop" is all the cash and markers that players present to the dealers in exchange for chips. The term comes from the dealer's (or boxman's) act of "dropping" cash through the slot in the table. As a percentage, it is *not* the same as "casino advantage," but is more correctly a measure of that portion of a player's stake that the player ultimately parts with.

The "casino advantage" (house edge) is that built-in percentage that works against the player on every bet, such as 1.41% on the dice table's pass line. As the player continues making bets, the casino advantage works away at him, increasing the casino's drop percentage. If the player has no concept of quitting, the casino eventually will have taken

when the Claridge was offering the public a four-deck game with surrender? Surprisingly, 99 percent of the answers were idiotic and ludicrous. One guy at a $100 minimum table told me that he didn't care about four, six or eight-decks. "The reason I play here," he said, "is because I always get a comp for a meal!"

"If you're looking for a meal and a card game," I said, "why don't you call Richard Simmons and play 'Deal-A-Meal?'"

I wanted to know Wagner's feelings on the subject of players and their knowledge of the games.

"The public, in general, is not totally aware of the rules of the games, particularly as it relates to shuffle, size of the deck, and the different options of the rules, especially in blackjack. Blackjack is the only game where the house advantage changes based on every card that's pulled out of the shoe. Some customers might be naive on that fact. There's only about ten percent of our customers that give a damn about the pricing (odds) of the games."

his entire stake, and the drop percentage for that particular player will be 100%.

Although often used interchangeably with "drop," the "hold" is that portion of *all bets made* that is not returned to the players. Casinos use the term, "handle," to refer to all bets made. It's interesting that casinos cannot measure the true "hold" at a table game because they have no idea what the handle is (how can they keep track of all bets made?). But they can keep a precise accounting at slot machines where each coin played is recorded. If 1,000 coins are played (the handle), and only 950 coins are paid out, that leaves 50 coins as the "hold," and a hold percentage of 5%. Unlike the drop percentage, the hold percentage will, over the long term, approximate the true casino advantage.

Framed pictures and personal memorabilia lined the walls and anchored the glass bookcase shelves in Wagner's office. A museum of memories that age the artist, but inspire the soul. Wagner, leaning back in his chair was silent. A moment of verbal truce. A time to reorganize his thoughts. Turning to me, Wagner said, "I think Perskie has opened the door giving us the best opportunity we'll ever have to change the regulations."

Wagner's voice went from optimistic to pessimistic. "And quite frankly," said Wagner, "I don't think the industry is going to do a good job in asking for what it needs."

I would like to thank Glenn Lillie, Vice President of Public Affairs, and his staff, for arranging my day with Roger Wagner.

Lillie introduced me to Robert Renneisen, Jr., Executive Vice President of Marketing and Casino Operations.* Renneisen, whose office is ten feet away from Wagner's, invited me in for an impromptu question and answer session.

When the Claridge decided that they wanted to be "more marketing driven," they reached out for the talents of Renneisen. His first objective was to change the image of the Claridge. His idea was to spotlight the intimacy and friendliness of the Claridge.

In Las Vegas, Renneisen worked for Caesars Palace and Ramada Inn's Tropicana. Comparing the two markets, Renneisen said, "It's an entirely different market. It's almost a different industry."

---

*Renneisen is now president of the Claridge, since Wagner's departure.

It seems like the casino industry is taking a new direction in the '90s. Many hotels have been streamlining their casino host staff. As VP of casino operations, I asked Renneisen how he views the high-roller market in Atlantic City, and at the Claridge.

"We don't compete very heavily for high rollers. We have some high rollers who happen to like the Claridge, but we don't go out of our way to compete with Caesars or Trump Plaza for the high-roller business. We're more of a middle-of-the-road kind of house."

Question: Lately, casinos have been saying that the "perks" they have to give to high-rollers don't justify the means. Do you agree with that?

Answer: "Yes, I do. The philosophy that Caesars operates under is very similar to ours. We're at the point now where we have fewer hosts than we did before. We like all the business we can get but, beyond a certain point, unless you have a lot of high rollers, if one comes in and beats you it takes a long time to recoup what we've lost. We don't win all the time."

Renneisen usually works six days a week. "It's not an eight-hour day," explained Renneisen, "but, we don't get paid eight-hour wages. You get a good salary in this business but you earn it!

"The surprising thing to a lot of people is that the president and senior officers of a casino, especially here in Atlantic City, really spend most of their day making the same kinds of decisions that any corporate executive makes. This one building is probably the equivalent of a Fortune 500 corporation, or close to it. You're talking about places that are a quarter of a billion dollar plus, per-year corporations. That's a departure from the way it used to be in Las Vegas.

"The head of a casino hotel used to be like the general manager of a hotel that had a casino in it. Today, you're dealing with people that are running two- or three-hundred-million-dollar-a-year businesses with more then 2,500 employees. The general manager of the best non-casino hotel in the country would probably be qualified to come in and be VP or director of hotel operations in a business like this."

"It seems to me," I commented, "that there's a big difference between a non-casino hotel and a casino. More than facts and figures, a casino president, in my opinion, should have a feel for a casino. A gut feeling about gamblers and the games."

"I think it takes that to do the job well," responded Renneisen. "If you look around this town I think you'll find that the majority of those who are in the top jobs *aren't* the kind of people that you're talking about. They tend to be more accountants or controllers. If you can identify those places that become the most successful over time, they are headed by leadership that does have a flair for the business. More than that, they have a flair of what this business should represent to the customer.

"People come here to experience something different, something that's exciting and something that they can't experience at home. The whole experience here is to create an escape. People come here to have fun and it's our job to make sure that they do. That's our mission."

Epilogue

"Atlantic City is no Las Vegas and never will be."

Las Vegas Review-Journal

In 1976, New Jersey voters approved casino gambling. The idea was to create a new source of revenue for the state, and to help Atlantic City become the tourist mecca that it once was. It was never the state's goal to become another Las Vegas.

A craps shooter once said, "Do you know what separates Las Vegas from Atlantic City? Three thousand miles!"

As the gambling industry in Atlantic City enters its adolescent years, it shows signs of maturity. This industry, once considered to be the "illegitimate son" of organized crime, is no longer up for adoption. Many of those who once opposed casino gambling have changed their attitudes. Commercial, corporate-run gambling, like state lotteries, has erased the so-called sleazy image.

No one anticipated the enormous economic impact that casino gambling has had on the state. Over a ten-year period, starting from its inception back in 1978, casinos paid $3.5 billion in federal, state, and local taxes. The work force of the industry numbers over 42,000. Tax revenues which help fund senior citizen programs and aid the disabled, amount to nearly $233 million annually.

Atlantic City is more than just facts and figures. The success of Atlantic City isn't found on some corporation's bottom line. The real prosperity is written on the faces of the people who come here. From the elderly couple on a fixed income, to the high roller with unlimited income. High roller, low roller, medium roller... they all roll into town for the same reason.

Atlantic City may never be another Las Vegas. But it will always reign as the Queen of Resorts!

A young boy, wearing a white summer suit, blue bow tie, and a new pair of Buster Browns, walks between his parents as they stroll the Boardwalk. Juggling a vanilla ice cream cone in one hand, and his mother's love in the other, he smiles, as the sights and sounds of a summer night go passing by.

Amusement piers, like anchored ships, harbor the shoreline. Kaleidoscope lights kidnap your imagination, and ransom your innocence. Echoing off the blue cathedral sky, there is music. An overture of hope and promise filters down the concert-hall Boardwalk. Pipe organ melodies with alluring harmonies captivate and charm a child's heart.

Children smile as they circle the world on the neon-lit carousel. Wooden horses, painted for the season and trained to be gentle, pace the merry-go-round circle. Mothers, dizzy with worry, wave as sons and daughters go spinning by.

When you're eight years old, life on the Boardwalk is an adventure. An unexplored wooden midway of enchantment and splendor. The doorway to an ocean of dreams where lighthouse eyes search for castaways lost at sea.

Eight years old, and your mind is like a sponge absorbing every drop of life. A fountain of memories that years later will quench our hearts when seasons of drought age our spirit.

Thirty-seven years ago, I was that eight-year-old boy.

Bibliography

Atlantic City Press, selected articles, 1974/90.

New York Times, selected articles, 1974/90.

Wall Street Journal, selected articles, 1974/90.

The Boardwalk Jungle, Ovid Demaris, Bantam Books, New York, N.Y., 1986.

U.S. News & World Report, selected articles, 1974/90.

Newsweek Magazine, selected articles, 1974/90.

Time Magazine, selected articles, 1974/90.

Forbes Magazine, selected articles, 1976/89.

Casino Journal, selected articles, 1988/90.

Player Magazine, selected articles, 1988/90.

Trump, The Art of The Deal, Donald J. Trump, Tony Schwartz, Warner Books, New York, N.Y., 1987.

Star-Ledger, selected articles, 1974/90.

New Jersey Monthly, selected articles, 1976/90.

Business Week, selected articles, 1974/90.

Grand Rapids Press, selected articles, 1990.

Million Dollar Blackjack, Ken Uston, SRS Enterprises, Inc., Hollywood, Ca., 1981.

Mensa Think-Smart Book, Dr. Abbie F. Salny, Lewis Burke Frumkes, Harper & Row, New York, N.Y., 1986.

All About Craps, John Gollehon, G.P. Putnam's Sons, New York, 1985.

Casino Games, John Gollehon, Gollehon Press, Inc., Grand Rapids, Michigan, 1986.

Pay The Line, John Gollehon, G.P. Putnam's Sons, New York, 1983.

Playboy Magazine, March 1990.

Philadelphia Magazine, May 1990.

Tell It To The King, Larry King and Peter Occhiogrosso, G.P. Putnam's & Sons, New York, N.Y., 1988.

Las Vegas Behind The Tables, Barney Vinson, Gollehon Press, Inc., Grand Rapids, Michigan, 1986.